Guidance from the Greatest

Guidance from the Greatest

What the World War Two generation
can teach us about how we live our lives

Gavin Mortimer

CONSTABLE

CONSTABLE

First published in Great Britain in 2020 by Constable

1 3 5 7 9 10 8 6 4 2

Copyright © Gavin Mortimer, 2020

The moral right of the author has been asserted.

A CIP catalogue record for this book
is available from the British Library.

ISBN: 978-1-47213-512-4 (hardback)

Typeset in Minion Pro by SX Composing DTP, Rayleigh, Essex
Printed and bound in Great Britain by Clays Ltd, Elcograf, S.p.A

Papers used by Constable are from well-managed forests
and other responsible sources.

To Bob and Bobbie,
whose wit, wisdom and warmth I miss

Acknowledgements

If the devil finds work for idle hands, then so did the lockdown, and this book is the result. Conceived midway through the unprecedented period, the book was written, edited and designed with a dynamism that was in marked contrast to the lethargic response of Britain's political class to the crisis.

For that, I am grateful to my agent, Matthew Hamilton, who recognised instantly the originality of the idea, and to Andreas Campomar at Constable, for his alacrity. Thanks, too, to Claire Chesser at Constable, for all her work, and my editor, Jon Davies, for doing a grand job so swiftly and so skilfully.

And that's it. Unusually for one of my books, there are no warm words for archivists, curators and librarians

– that's not because we've fallen out, but because they've been closed for months.

Fortunately, over the decades I have accumulated a huge amount of material from more than 200 interviews with the men and women of the Greatest Generation, and that, along with a similar number of letters and personal papers provided to me in response to advertisements placed in magazines and newspapers, was a rich mine. Nearly all of the interviewees and correspondents are dead – and I was saddened to hear of Dame Vera Lynn's death just days after I had described in the book the delightful day I spent in her company in 2004.

She belonged to a magnificent generation and I feel privileged to have met so many, and to have been so enriched and inspired by their courage, integrity and humility.

Gavin Mortimer
June 2020

Contents

Introduction

On 23 March 2020, Prime Minister Boris Johnson gave an unprecedented address to the British people in response to the global COVID-19 pandemic. 'The time has come for us all to do more,' announced the PM. 'From this evening, I must give the British people a very simple instruction: You must stay at home.'

The three-month lockdown that ensued was arguably Britain's gravest crisis since the Second World War. One member of the Government, Health Secretary Matt Hancock, invoked the Blitz spirit of 1940 as he attempted to rally the nation: 'Despite the pounding every night, the rationing, the loss of life, they pulled together in one gigantic national effort,' he said. 'Today, our generation is facing its own test, fighting a very real and new disease.'

There was one essential difference – in 1940, there was bold leadership but, in 2020, the Government was indecisive and diffident and, as a result, they struggled to inspire much confidence in the people. It was a case of Lions led by Dunces.

Each week brought new and confusing amendments to the Health Protection (COVID-19 Restrictions) Regulations 2020, some of which even one Tory MP, Tobias Ellwood, admitted were 'ridiculous'. Social 'bubble' rules were baffling and, at one point, intimacy was illegal. As one headline in *The Australian* newspaper put it: 'NO SEX PLEASE, WE'RE BRITISH: BORIS JOHNSON'S VIRUS BONK BAN'. The befuddlement continued as the country emerged from the lockdown: should face masks be worn and why were men allowed to have their beards trimmed at the barbers but women couldn't have their eyebrows waxed at the hairdressers?

The Mayor of London confessed that the lockdown had left him feeling 'fragile' and, as a result, there were days when he was not 'providing proper leadership', which rang true of most of the Establishment. There was the scandalous mismanagement of the crisis in care homes and the powers-that-be couldn't even agree to work together to reopen the schools, so there was the embarrassing sight of theme parks and zoos welcoming children in June . . . but not their schools.

One person who rose to the occasion to remind the nation of the traits that make us collectively tick was the Queen. In only her fifth non-Christmas address to the nation in her sixty-eight-year reign, Her Majesty the Queen told a television audience of twenty-four million to draw on the 'attributes of self-discipline, of quiet, good-humoured resolve'. By doing so, promised the Queen, 'we will overcome it [and] I hope in the years to come, everyone will be able to take pride in how they responded to this challenge, and those who come after us will say the Britons of this generation were as strong as any.'

No one displayed this 'quiet, good-humoured resolve' more than Tom Moore. Like Her Majesty, Captain Tom is one of 'Churchill's children', the generation born in the 1920s and who helped defeat the evil of Nazism. Captain Tom (or Colonel, to give him his new rank) raised nearly £33 million during the lockdown by completing 100 laps of his garden on his walking frame while wearing his regimental blazer and wartime medals, awarded for his service with the Duke of Wellington's Regiment. 'You've got to be optimistic, to think that things will get better,' said the 100-year-old Moore, when asked by Platinum Skies Retirement Living for the secret of his longevity.

It was a mindset he had cultivated as a young soldier. 'It's part of the adventure of life,' he said in response to a question about his war service. 'I don't recall ever being frightened. Maybe I should have been! But we survived. I look back on my service in the army as a very enjoyable time and I still think about it now. There was so much comradeship between us.'

The optimism and indomitability of Tom Moore lifted the country and stiffened the sinews of the weary as the lockdown took an emotional toll on a nation not used to being deprived of its liberty. Also doing her bit to lift spirits was Dame Vera Lynn, the Forces' Sweetheart of the Second World War, who found herself back in the charts after the Queen referenced her song 'We'll Meet Again' in her address to the nation.

Dame Vera Lynn died in June at the age of 103 and her passing made all the front pages. As the *Daily Telegraph* reflected in its obituary, 'Vera Lynn seemed a symbol of much that the nation wished it had retained.'

In the Second World War, she had sung to packed audiences in the London Palladium during the Blitz and, later, she toured the Far East, putting on dozens of morale-boosting shows for troops in India and Burma. Speaking shortly before her death, Dame Vera urged the country to stay positive: 'Don't give up hope – times may be tough but they will get better.'

But hold on! Before we get too sentimental about the Second World War (and, in the process, run ourselves down), it's worth pointing out that, in the 1930s, the so-called 'Greatest Generation' were regarded as the 'Slackest Generation'. One of these 'slackers', Richard Hillary, an Oxford student before enlisting as an RAF fighter pilot, admitted in his wartime memoir that he and his peers

'. . . were disillusioned and spoiled . . . superficially we were selfish and egocentric, without any Holy Grail in which we could lose ourselves.'

David Lloyd George, the Prime Minister from 1916–22, agreed. In mourning the passing of the Victorian social reformer John Clifford in 1936, Lloyd George said he was 'an example to a soft, slack and self-indulgent generation of what can be achieved by courage, resolution, hard work and consecration to duty'.

Lloyd George died in March 1945, just weeks before the 'Soft Slackers' helped apply the *coup de grace* to Hitler's Third Reich twelve years into what the Führer had boasted would be a 1,000-year reign. Through the courage, resolution, hard work and consecration to duty that Lloyd George didn't believe they possessed, they became immortalised as the 'Greatest Generation'.

Do those qualities remain? Yes, judging by the response of millions of Brits during the COVID-19 crisis. Key workers on the frontline, particularly doctors and nurses, displayed plenty of Brit Grit, as did those stuck at home, who were forced to adapt to a new way of life. Despite being cut off physically from family and friends, people came together to support the elderly and the vulnerable, while others raised money for the NHS in a variety of ingenious ways. In the words of Dame Vera: 'I think we have seen a great sense of community and friendship return to our cities, towns and villages.'

This book is a celebration of those British qualities that rarely receive much attention – stoicism, self-discipline and selflessness aren't, to slip into modern parlance, very 'sexy'. Yet they are essential traits of the British character, all of them embodied by Tom Moore. 'Before World War Two, there was a certain degree of poverty and people were finding life very difficult,' he said at the height of the COVID-19 crisis. 'At the present time, people are still finding it difficult, but it's not as hard now as it was then. We still need to continue this life with hope and think that tomorrow is going to be as good a day as possible.'

I've never met Colonel Tom but I have interviewed scores of his generation, men and women who came through the war and considered themselves better people for the experience. There was plenty of terror and tragedy for soldiers, sailors, air crew and civilians, but that wasn't what stuck in the minds of the men and women to whom I spoke. 'During all those years, there was such a good community spirit about and neighbours helped each other when someone was bombed and everyone rallied round to find things for them,' one survivor of the Blitz told me. 'And there was always a cup of tea for whoever needed one.'

That may sound trite, but it's also the truth. There was a flame of fellowship among the Greatest Generation that was never extinguished and, while today it may not burn as brightly in their descendants, we can still use it as a guiding light as we go forward into an uncertain future.

1

Stoicism

My acquaintance with Beryl Waterman began in 2013 with an indignant letter. She was miffed that I had omitted her husband, John, from my book about the Special Boat Squadron (SBS) during the Second World War. I was abashed to admit I had no knowledge of John, who had served in the SBS as a wireless operator for two years and subsequently emigrated to Canada.

Delighted to have found another member of the dwindling band of SBS veterans, I included John in the second edition of the book. I also learned about Beryl's service in the Women's Auxiliary Air Force (WAAF), a branch of the service whose contribution to the war effort Beryl felt had been neglected.

The WAAF was established in 1939 and, at its peak in

1943, had 182,000 personnel. Although they didn't fly, the WAAFs performed vital functions, ranging from crewing barrage balloons to aircraft maintenance to parachute packing to plotting the path of enemy aircraft and working with codes and ciphers. 'Day in, day out, they diligently did their duty,' states the Royal Air Force Museum. 'Great strength of character was required by many WAAFs in continuing to work despite the loss of friends and loved ones.'

Eighteen-year-old Beryl Blackett, as she was in 1942, worked as a plotter in the Fighter Command Operations Room of RAF Ouston in County Durham. She had joined the WAAFs as soon as she came of age, much to the chagrin of her father, who had wangled Beryl a 'beastly job in the tax office' in the hope it would deter her from enlisting.

Plotting was demanding work and, in her free time, Beryl and her fellow WAAFs would let their hair down in the local pub, the Lion and Lamb. One evening in 1942, she met a twenty-year-old Spitfire pilot called Malcolm 'Robbie' Robertson, a New Zealander who had volunteered for the RAF six weeks after turning eighteen.

Malcolm and Beryl fell in love. For both, it was their first serious relationship and the war made their love all the more intense. In October 1942, Robbie was posted 100 miles north to RAF Drem in Scotland, but he and Beryl wrote nearly every day and, in November, they enjoyed an innocent weekend together. Their next rendezvous was planned for the middle of January; both had wangled a 48-hour leave pass and they arranged to meet in Edinburgh.

On the afternoon of 16 January, Beryl telephoned RAF Drem to tell Robbie she was about to leave for Edinburgh. But she didn't speak to her boyfriend; instead, Beryl was connected to an orderly who informed her that Sergeant Pilot Malcolm Robertson had been killed in a crash earlier that day.

Beryl spent her 48 hours' leave grieving. Then it was back to the Fighter Command Operations Room. There was the odd word of sympathy, but what was one more death among the dozens every day?

Robbie's remains weren't discovered until the summer of 2012, disinterred from a hillside in the Scottish borders by an aviation archaeologist. At a depth of 18ft, he and his team detected the heavy odour of petrol and then heard the clang of metal as their excavator struck the crushed remains of Spitfire AR403, which had last been seen plummeting towards the ground 69 years earlier. The crash was attributed to pilot error.

The aircraft surrendered its secret slowly: the control column minus the spade grip . . . the compass . . . the lower part of the gun sight . . . the pilot's rubber dinghy . . . Robbie's baling-out bucket . . . his parachute release buckle . . . a map case . . . and part of his armoured head rest. And then what remained of Robbie, which amounted to a few bone fragments, some strips of his flying uniform and his shoes.

A local newspaper reported the discovery and one of Beryl's daughters, Jane, read the story online. The pilot fitted the description of Mum's first boyfriend. Beryl was shocked when she learned they'd found Robbie. She and John had been married for seven decades but first love is never forgotten. 'Robbie was such fun,' Beryl told me. 'He had a lovely sense of humour and I was so smitten. I was absolutely shattered to learn of his death.'

She showed me his photograph and his correspondence, and a letter of condolence from Robbie's wing commander. It was difficult to read all of his words because the ink had been smudged from the tears of a heartbroken eighteen-year-old.

* * *

The stoicism of Beryl was commonplace in the Second World War, particularly among women, whose war was one of passivity for the most part, compared to their menfolk, and for that reason their mental fortitude was all the more impressive.

My grandfather sailed from England for India with the RAF in 1942, and returned home nearly four years later. His wife and four-year-old son received the occasional censored letter but, to all intents and purposes, he was removed from their lives and, when he did come back, it took some readjustment to resume family life.

Like a lot of young soldiers, Arthur [Tommo] Thomson hurriedly married his sweetheart not long into the war. He then volunteered for the commandos and later served for three years in the SAS, fighting in North Africa, Sicily, Italy, France and then Germany, where he was among the first SAS soldiers to enter Belsen concentration camp in April 1945. 'It took me the best part of two years to get back to sanity in civilian life,' Tommo told me. 'I used to wake up in the morning screaming. My wife couldn't stand it; in fact, she left me to go and live with my sister for a week. I was a madman. It suddenly subsided but it took over a year to become normal.' Tommo and his wife remained together until her death in 1984.

Jean Switters, a Belgian who served in the SAS and married an Englishwoman, also suffered psychologically upon his return. When I interviewed the Switters in 2002, Jean described how for about a year after the war he sat in an armchair twirling a bunch of keys on his finger. He barely spoke to his wife. The agony was immense for her. She had her husband back, but only physically. Emotionally, he was still fighting his war. But she was patient and loving and stoic, and one morning, like Tommo, Jean returned to her emotionally.

* * *

Since the 1960s, it's been fashionable to mock the stoicism of the Greatest Generation. It began with the iconoclastic Beyond the Fringe and a series of nasty, sneering skits about the 'stiff upper lip' of the Second World War. The satirists were from Oxbridge, the milieu that in the 1930s had been open in its contempt of Britain and which, even when war began, was ambivalent about where its loyalties lay, such was their disdain for British culture.

But Beyond the Fringe quickly became the darlings of the cultural élite, as did Monty Python, also Oxbridge comedians who mocked the stoicism of their parents. Throughout the 1970s and 1980s, disdain for the Greatest Generation was *de rigueur* and, in twenty-first-century Britain, a 'stiff upper lip' has become a pejorative term, another way of saying someone is emotionally retarded.

In 2012, the broadcaster Ian Hislop made a programme examining the subject – *Stiff Upper Lip: an Emotional History of Britain* – in which he said, 'The rapid social change of the 1960s left the stiff upper lip looking old-fashioned, and even more so when the "me generation" embraced therapy and "letting it all hang out".'

But Hislop claimed stoicism was still a British trait, and gave as evidence the hardiness of the public in enduring wet weather to watch the Royal Flotilla on the Thames during the Diamond Jubilee of 2012. 'Over centuries, the British have come to be seen by others and to see themselves in terms of reserve, resilience and restraint,' he said.

That stereotype wasn't always on display during the COVID-19 crisis. The singer Sam Smith, an idol to millions, wept hot tears of frustration because life had become a little boring (although they later claimed it was a joke) and it wasn't an edifying sight to see shoppers stripping supermarket shelves of essential items, among which, bizarrely, were loo rolls. Nonetheless, great swathes of the country accepted the loss of their liberty stoically, even if they felt that the Government had cracked under pressure from scientists and broadcasters. In that sense, there was a parallel to the Second World War. Back then, politicians, intellectuals and military experts had spouted ominous warnings for years about the destruction they envisaged from aerial attack in the event of a conflict.

The catalyst for the scaremongering was the bombing of the Spanish town of Guernica in 1937 by German aircraft. The Government assembled a team of experts – the Committee of Imperial Defence – which made one inaccurate estimate after another in the eighteen months before war was declared (a bit like Imperial College did with COVID-19). As a result, the Ministry of Health extrapolated these figures to forecast that 600,000 Britons would die in the first six months of the aerial war, with a further 1.2

million wounded. The government panicked – where would they bury the dead? Where would they treat the wounded? How would they deal with the homeless? What could they do to prevent a gas attack?

Pamphlets warning what to do in the event of devastating air raids were distributed to households, along with gas masks, and there was, said George Orwell, 'a defeatist' attitude among the intelligentsia. So, too, in Whitehall, recalled John Colville, a young member of the Ministry of Economic Warfare in 1939. On 3 September that year, he returned home 'reflecting that we seemed remarkably ill-prepared for Armageddon'.

While the élite prepared for the worst, the rest of the country kept calm and carried on. Colville was still braced for Armageddon on 10 September and admitted to his diary that he was surprised by the stoicism of the general public. 'There is nothing about the gaily dressed, smiling crowds in the streets to remind us of this great catastrophe,' he wrote, 'except perhaps for the gas masks slung across their backs.'

George Orwell refused to carry a gas mask and so, in his observation, did 80 per cent of Londoners. 'The assumption was that a person who carried a gas mask was of the ultra-cautious type,' he wrote in his diary in June 1940. 'The suburban ratepayer'.

Bravado, of course, is easy when there are no bullets or bombs flying around, but it remained the prevailing attitude among the public even after the start of the Battle of Britain in July 1940. Dogfights in the skies over southern England became an entertainment sport. John Colville wrote in his diary on 31 July that, in recent days, Dover pier had been crammed with people craning their necks to watch the RAF take on the Luftwaffe. 'It is encouraging that their passion for sightseeing should still be greater than that for self-preservation,' wrote Colville.

In the middle of August, the Germans began bombing ports and industrial cities, and there were also light raids on some London suburbs. The people were thrilled. Orwell couldn't believe his eyes, as he wrote in his diary on 16 August. 'Everyone's behaviour is foolish in the extreme,' he said, describing the response to air-raid sirens. 'For the first fifteen seconds, there is great alarm, blowing of whistles and shouts to children to go indoors, then people begin to congregate on the streets and gaze expectantly at the sky. In the daytime, people are apparently ashamed to go into the shelters 'til they hear the bombs.'

What they needed, said Orwell, who despite his claims to the contrary had a touch of the defeatist about him at this time, was 'one real raid to teach them how to behave'.

Londoners got that raid on 7 September 1940, and one thereafter every day or night until 3 November, but still Britons didn't behave as Orwell wanted. Nor did the raids – as the doom-monger Orwell predicted in his diary on 10 September – 'break down everyone's morale'.

For all his time spent observing the English working class, the middle-class Orwell never really understood what made them tick. He would have been flabbergasted to read some of the memories relayed to me in letters from working-class Londoners who lived through the Blitz.

Iris Strange, for example, was a young East Ender in 1940. 'One particular night as we were about to have our fish and chips, the air-raid siren went,' she wrote to tell me in 2004. 'My dad piled up all the meals on a tray and we proceeded to go down to the Anderson shelter. It was pouring with rain and Dad put up a huge umbrella and then put on his bowler hat. My mum raised her fist in the air and shouted, "You're not going to stop me eating my fish and chips, Mr Hitler!" When I look back and think about it, I have to laugh.'

Lillian Patient was working in the Lyons' teashop near the Blackwall Tunnel on the afternoon of Saturday, 7 September, the day 350 Luftwaffe bombers attacked Britain in the first major raid of what came to be called the Blitz. 'My job was to put up the shutters over the front of the windows of the shop as soon as the alarm went,' explained Lillian. 'Looking up in the sky, I saw a formation of German bombers . . . and made for the staff shelter in the backyard of the shop. The staff were already there and one of the Nippies (waitresses) was playing the mouth organ. We had some knees-up!'

Billie Hill was a teenage telephonist for the General Post Office (GPO). 'It is rather difficult to recall everything that happened, but we seemed to just take a deep breath and get on with our work,' she said of life during the Blitz.

During the Second World War, 60,595 Britons were killed as a result of German air raids and 86,182 were seriously wounded. Many more suffered emotional scars. Florence Rumford, a nurse at a first-aid post in Shoreditch during the Blitz, wrote to me in 2004, to admit, 'Even now, after all these years, the siren from police or ambulances still sends a shudder through me . . . Nothing can explain the awful crump and the crashing, the long time as everything fell and crumpled around you, and then the relief that still you weren't buried and can breathe.'

For Florence, as for everyone who lived through the Blitz, there were moments of absolute terror impossible to describe to those who haven't suffered the same experience. Nevertheless, explained Florence, 'I'm still in contact with one of my fellow nurses, and we often talk on the phone but seldom discuss the bad bits, and often laugh at the funny bits.'

This stoicism wasn't unique to London. Elaine Kidwell of Swansea took pride in the fact that at seventeen she was one of the youngest air-raid wardens in the country. When her city was attacked on 19 February 1941, she was caught in the blast of a bomb. 'I hit a wall,' she recalled. 'Amazingly,

I was all right so I dusted my jacket down and applied my lipstick. My lipstick was like my armour, so I felt safer.'

Lipstick on a stiff upper lip, what mirth that would have aroused among the smug satirists of Beyond the Fringe. They could have included it as one of their 'Aftermyth of War' sketches, alongside their 'Futile Gesture' skit, which lampooned the stoicism of RAF pilots. Men like John Freeborn, DFC, who flew more operational hours in his Spitfire during the Battle of Britain than any other pilot. John was a down-to-earth Yorkshireman, not at all the plummy-voiced airman portrayed by Beyond the Fringe. He lost most of his friends in the Battle of Britain. 'You had to become callous and indifferent to death,' John told me. 'Of course, you were very sorry, particularly if they were close to you, but you got on with it.'

The young satirists of the early 1960s were anti-Establishment, and who could blame them at that time with the patrician Victorian Harold Macmillan running the country? But the mordant wit of Beyond the Fringe went beyond the Tory Establishment and targeted British culture and character in general.

Yet when Hong Kong 'Flu swept Britain in the winter of 1968–69, killing an estimated 30,000, the Greatest Generation was now in charge. The Labour Health Minister, David Ennals, had fought in North Africa and Normandy, and the Chancellor of the Exchequer, Roy Jenkins, had been a Bletchley Park codebreaker. Their measured response to the virus filtered down to the public at large. 'People are realising that it is only a mild illness and, in many cases, medical advice is not necessary,' a Midland GP told the *Birmingham Daily Post* at the height of the epidemic. 'They are helping us by not panicking.'

British people didn't really panic during the COVID-19 crisis, despite the fact that the mismanagement of the pandemic by the authorities deprived them of their freedom and also essential services such as GPs and dentists. In several cases, Brits were forced to take matters – or rather their teeth – into their own hands. One man from Devon, Billy Taylor, told the BBC how he spent an hour and a half removing a rotten tooth with a pair of pliers; a woman from Yorkshire plucked out her troublesome tooth with a kitchen knife and dental floss.

But if the British people have a stiff (if a little blooded) upper lip, the same can't be said for the ruling class.

From the late 1980s onwards, cultural and increasingly political power passed from the Greatest Generation into the hands of a new generation, whose characters had not been forged by hardship or adversity. Stoicism was not their strong suit.

Parliament had continued to sit during the Blitz, their only concession to the air attacks to alter the hours of business from 2.45pm until late at night to 11.00am to

5.00pm, and to move from the Palace of Westminster to Church House, just a few hundred yards away. Even those changes were greeted with dismay by many MPs, who saw them as excessively cautious, but there was never any question of suspending Parliament, as happened for a month in March 2020 when COVID-19 succeeded where the Luftwaffe had failed.

In explaining why Parliament was taking a break, Speaker Sir Lindsay Hoyle wrote in *The House* magazine: 'I hope that when this historic crisis passes and we return to business as usual, we will come back stronger.'

'Business as usual' was an expression coined by Londoners during the Blitz; it was a message to Hitler – do your worst, but the city will carry on regardless. As one shopkeeper wrote on a sign outside his damaged store: 'You can break our windows but not our spirit'.

Sir Lindsay's use of the term merely drew attention to the pusillanimity of Parliament in 2020. But we should not have been surprised, for stoicism among the political and media class is rare in this day and age.

Its demise began in 1997 when Princess Diana died in a car crash and the press vilified the Queen for not emoting with the rest of the country, for adhering to her lifelong motto of 'never complain, never explain'; in other words, being stoic in the face of tragedy.

The 'Dianafication of Britain' revolutionised the media

and ushered in the end of factual reporting. Ever since the news media has prioritised emotion over facts in its reporting, feeding on the culture of 'safetyism' that dominates Britain's Establishment. As the BBC broadcaster Andrew Marr wrote in his book, *My Trade*: 'To sell papers, news must move and often that means provoking fear.' Never was this more evident than during COVID-19, with broadcasters and newspapers running one scare story after another.

In 1993, the author George MacDonald Fraser wrote his war memoir, *Quartered Safe Out Here*, a gripping account of serving as an infantryman in Burma. Post-war Fraser made his fortune with the creation of the Victorian anti-hero, Lord Flashman, but nothing made him prouder than his service with the Border Regiment, a teenage middle-class Scot among tough working-class Cumbrians.

Several of them were killed and, after each death, the soldier's military effects were divided among his pals. 'It was part of war,' wrote Fraser. 'The celebrated British stiff upper lip, the resolve to conceal emotion which is not only embarrassing and useless, but harmful, is just plain common sense. But that was half a century ago. Things are different now, when the media seems to feel they have a duty to dwell on emotion, the more harrowing the better, and to encourage its indulgence . . . the obscene intrusion is justified as "caring" and "compassionate" when it is the exact opposite.'

John Waterman turned 99 during the COVID-19 crisis. He's been suffering from ill health of late but he celebrated his birthday with a wee dram and with Beryl at his side, as stoic and as unflappable as ever, despite the threat from the virus. As their daughter Jane remarked to me, 'Their generation seems to be a lot tougher than mine!'

2

Fellowship

I first visited the Morvan, in the Bourgogne region of France, in July 2002. On a high summer's day it looked an enchanted land of hills, forests, valleys and lakes. The Morvan is approximately twice the size of the Lake District, a wilderness untainted by motorways and high-speed rail links.

The people are generous and unsophisticated, welcoming and hardy. The purpose of my visit was to follow in the footsteps of the Special Air Service (SAS), a squadron of which had parachuted into the Morvan in June 1944 and spent three months fighting a guerrilla war against the Germans.

Two ancient Maquisards, André and René, were my guides. Although grey and stooped, they were still full of energy and we drove deep into the forest of Montsauche along a rough track in a pick-up truck. It was a track that André in particular knew well; a mechanic by trade, he had been a Maquis driver during the war.

Eventually, the trail became impassable and we continued on foot, heading deeper into the forest upon a carpet of pine needles. As we walked, André and René pointed out sites of interest: the Maquis camp; the SAS camp; and the crude hospital where doctor Alec Prochiantz extracted bullets from wounds using the most rudimentary of surgical instruments. His wife, Edmée, was his assistant; after the war, she received the King's Medal for Courage in the Cause of Freedom, one of only 3,200 such medals bestowed by George VI. Edmée's citation praised her 'extraordinary standard of courage and fine sense of duty, and the SAS troops owed a great deal of gratitude to this gallant lady'.

The Maquis cemetery was at the top of a steep path and the graves of the Frenchmen lay among the trees. At the rear of the cemetery were two plaques bearing the names of Alex Muirhead and Frederick 'Chalky' White, and on each plaque was the regimental badge of the SAS.

Muirhead and White had parachuted into the Morvan in June 1944, members of A Squadron 1SAS, whose mission – codenamed Operation Houndsworth – was to arm and train the Maquis and then together attack enemy communications.

Chalky had landed on the roof of a house and put out his back. It was a couple of weeks before he was on his feet, and then almost immediately he was shot in the leg and elbow and lost three of his fingers in a short and very sharp encounter with a convoy of Germans. As one of his comrades wrote home to his girlfriend a day later: 'The man's positively inhuman.'

On each occasion, Chalky was nursed back to health by the Maquis and, when he died in 1995, he had requested that his ashes be spread in the cemetery deep inside the forest of Montsauche. So did Alex Muirhead, A Squadron's mortar officer, when he died in 1999.

Fourteen years earlier, Muirhead had compiled a report of Operation Houndsworth that he distributed among veterans of the mission. It was the prelude to a pilgrimage to the Morvan that subsequently became an annual event. In 1994, to mark the fiftieth anniversary, veterans from the SAS and the Maquis drank wine from bottles engraved with their emblems and the words 'We'll Never Forget'.

In his introduction to his report, Muirhead wrote: 'It is impossible to forget the bravery and kindness of the people of the Morvan who, in spite of great personal danger, with their villages burnt, men shot and women raped, supplied aid and food when necessary, and never betrayed us. Their pain, suffering and glory united the people of France and England in the Morvan in 1944.'

In 2005, the ashes of a third veteran were scattered in the Maquis cemetery, those of Captain Fraser McLuskey, the SAS padre in 1944. In 1951, he had written a memoir of his three months in the Morvan in which he wrote of the 'charm and attractiveness of the French character, the courage and the loyal friendship of the country people among whom we lived, and the Maquis among whom we worked'.

André and René were present when the padre's ashes were scattered, as was Alec Prochiantz, who had travelled to the Morvan from his home in Paris. 'In the summer of 1944, Fraser McLuskey discovered the reality of the cruelty of the German repressions, and he came to appreciate the warmth and patriotism of the Morvan people,' he said in his eulogy. 'We are now proud to be able to receive the ashes of our British friend.'

René also spoke at the ceremony: 'There is no bigger and moving proof of the fellowship of the padre than to ask to rest for eternity in the Morvan under the foliage that sheltered the Maquis and SAS.'

Fraser McLuskey's wartime memoir, *The Parachute Padre*, is atypical in that it is as much a spiritual journey as it is a war story. His focus is kinship and not killing. He was posted to the SAS in the spring of 1944, shortly after their return from operations in Sicily and Italy. They were based in McLuskey's native Scotland undergoing a rigorous retraining prior to parachuting into Occupied France. When they weren't training, they were roistering. 'It must be admitted, too, that at unit celebrations too much drink was consumed too often by too few,' wrote the padre. 'It must, on the other hand, be claimed that these parties were themselves the product of a fellowship that was genuine and sincere, a fellowship that is in our reunions still.'

More than fifty years after the padre wrote those words, he led the SAS in prayer at a service of dedication in St Columba's Church in London. Too poorly to attend in person, Fraser spoke from his home in Edinburgh and the sight and sound of him was the highlight of the service for the dozens of wartime veterans among the congregation.

One of those present was Bob Francis, who had parachuted into the Morvan as a member of a small reinforcement party for A Squadron. Among the reception committee was Fraser McLuskey, and for nineteen-year-old Bob, untested in combat, the presence of the padre was a source of comfort. Bob died of cancer six months before Fraser's passing and, in a final letter of farewell dictated two days before his death, Bob said: 'I wish to take this opportunity to say how much I have valued your friendship, some of which has lasted over seventy years . . . I say goodbye with love, sincere fraternal greetings, and affection to my old comrades at arms.'

* * *

The fellowship of the SAS was, of course, replicated in myriad other combat units throughout the Second World War. Mike Carr, one of the handful of veterans from the Long Range Desert Group, said it was a 'privilege' to serve in the unit. 'The camaraderie was magnificent . . . it was a family.'

In a letter he wrote to his mother in the event of his death, Captain Jocelyn Nicholls of No 7 Commando said he was not at all 'gloomy' at the prospect of death. 'I know it's not the thing to say, but I have loved the war; I have had with me for nearly two years of it the finest lot of chaps a man could wish to command. We've been through quite a lot together, and have a mutual respect and comradeship that nothing in this world can break. Together, we fear nothing in this world or the next.' Captain Nicholls was killed leading his men into action in Burma in 1942.

Ronald Searle's war was not glorious, but he recognised the camaraderie of which Jocelyn Nicholls talked. Captured in 1942, Ronald was sent to Changi to work on the infamous Death Railway between Burma and Thailand. Men died every day, often reduced by hunger and exhaustion to a sick pile of skin and bones. Ronald flirted with death but survived. 'The fellow feeling was absolutely fabulous,' he recalled, when he appeared on BBC radio's *Desert Island*

Discs in 2005. 'One thing that one learned was that human beings can be so marvellous to each other . . . under these circumstances, survival really depended on the attachment you had with your fellow prisoners.'

This fellowship existed also on the home front; it is what makes the Second World War unique. While there were a few Zeppelin raids on Britain in the First World War, the country's women and youngsters were, for the most part, distant bystanders. In 1939, millions of civilians volunteered their services in one capacity or another – old soldiers came out of retirement to form the Home Guard, adolescents were recruited as firewatchers, the Women's Land Army dug, milked and harvested and the emergency services were flooded with eager young men and women willing to drive ambulances or crew fire engines.

'Even the minority, which regards war as a crime and opposed this one to the moment of its outbreak, has no desire to run away,' wrote the pacifist author Vera Brittain in the summer 1940. 'Its members prefer to remain and share their country's fortunes; to assume the responsibility for these all the more when, for a time, they happen to be adverse; to perform the outstanding duties of detached thought and humanitarian co-operation; to serve – not war – but their fellow men.'

When the Blitz began on 7 September 1940, George Orwell immediately detected a difference in those around him. 'It was noticeable that people were much readier than before to talk to strangers in the street,' he wrote in his diary on 12 September.

Nonetheless, one should be wary of sentimentalising the war. There were plenty of working-class Britons who didn't think much of the Government or the Royal Family. A lot of Londoners in particular were, at best, ambivalent about the king and queen and, at worst, antagonistic, even after Buckingham Palace was bombed and the Queen's comment about now being able to 'look the East End in the face'.

Similarly, there was a rise in crime during the blackout and, once the air raids began, looters proliferated, a small number of whom were firefighters. Churchill even suppressed on occasions newspaper stories of such incidents because he didn't wish to damage the perception that all firemen were 'heroes with grimy faces'.

Fellowship – or, as George Orwell put it in an article for the *Daily Express* on 23 July 1941, the cry of 'we-are-all-in-it-together' – was noticeably absent among a tranche of the wealthy élite. If you had the money, he wrote, petrol and certain foods were obtainable, making a mockery of the declaration that Britain was experiencing an 'equality of sacrifice'. Other members of this social class fled London; by March 1940, the population of Chelsea had dropped from 57,000 to 36,000, which caused a problem when the Blitz began because many properties had no water as they had been cut off. So an over-stretched fire service had to divert resources to battle blazes in empty mansions.

But, overwhelmingly, the predominant spirit in London and across the rest of the country was one of fellowship. After Coventry was blitzed on 15 November 1940, the city's Bishop, Mervyn Haigh, addressed the congregation at a mass burial of the dead. 'This raid has brought us together in a common bond,' he told mourners. 'We are now better friends and neighbours than we were. Let us love and even live in the strength of this new faith. Let us go out and try to live unembittered lives.'

Towns in the countryside reached out to their city bretheren. In Marlow, Buckinghamshire, some local women opened the 'Cosy Corner Club', one of many such organisations to spring up across Britain. It was for mothers and children who had lost their homes in the London Blitz. 'A friendly atmosphere prevails . . . difficulties and misunderstandings which once loomed large have disappeared, and mothers and children alike look upon the "Cosy Corner Club" as a happy meeting ground,' reported the *West London Observer* newspaper in April 1941. 'The club offers a hearty welcome to any evacuee of whatever nationality, race or religion, especially to those who may be feeling lonely and in need of simple helpful friendship.'

There were similar centres in London for bombed-out families. Initially, the sheer scale of devastation caused by the raids led to criticism from the press and John Colville,

Churchill's private secretary, was involved in improving the rest centres. He visited one such centre in a Kentish Town school on 9 October 1940 and found the sleeping and sanitary arrangements inadequate. The food was good, he wrote in his diary, but what left an indelible impression was the camaraderie. 'There was a piano playing and the people were dancing, the atmosphere is one of willingness to be helpful and of sympathy,' he wrote in his diary. 'There are few complaints and the cheerfulness of the homeless, as of the staff, is remarkable.'

This fellowship was conveyed to me in countless letters I received when I wrote about the London Blitz in 2004. I kept the letters, like the one from Kathleen Urry, who wrote: 'During all those years there was such a good community spirit about and neighbours helped each other when someone was bombed and everyone rallied round to find things for them.'

And that of Patricia Morton, who recalled 'the marvellous atmosphere everywhere. I can feel it now, just thinking about it. You knew that everyone was doing their best to win the war . . . it was great.'

Edith Wood explained, 'I can remember very clearly the number of times walking to work and being given a lift by an army lorry with room to spare. I would not have missed those years for anything, and I feel very proud to have experienced the trials and tribulations and survived.'

Joyce Hancock described the atmosphere as 'marvellous . . . people helped each other'.

And Tom Winter told me he considered himself blessed 'to have lived through a time in history when people on the whole were good, decent and much more socially conscious of their fellow man'. The country, in his opinion, had a 'spiritual wealth' during the Second World War.

* * *

On the surface, there doesn't appear to be much 'spiritual wealth' left in the bank as far as Britain is concerned. If Brexit wasn't divisive enough, COVID-19 created further divisions between 'covidiots' and 'coronaphobics'; key workers and WFH (work from home); furloughed and non-furloughed. Then came June and the confrontations between statue demolishers and statue defenders.

Yet these are the divisions reported in the national media and amplified on social media; call them 'clickbait' divisions, if you will. Away from the febrile headlines, there is still a strong fellowship in Britain, and it emerged during COVID-19. When in March the NHS called for an army of volunteer responders, 750,000 offered their services – three times the number required. In the months that followed, they delivered medicines from chemists, drove patients to appointments and transported medical supplies for the NHS.

Many did their bit for their fellow citizens in other ways, like the people of Darlington who raised £100,000 for St Teresa's Hospice, or Daksha Varsani and Paresh Jethwa who, with a team of volunteers, founded the Community Response Kitchen in north-west London to create and deliver meals to overworked medical staff in local hospitals.

Of course, the challenge in 2020 was to foster fellowship while socially distancing – not an obstacle that had to be overcome in the Blitz. On the contrary, there was no keeping one's distance in the air-raid shelters when the Luftwaffe arrived – terrified people huddled together for comfort amidst the whine, whistle and bang of the enemy bombs.

During COVID-19, people had to encourage each other from a respectable distance, yet despite this restriction millions still got together on 8 May to mark the 75th anniversary of VE Day. Up and down the country, there were variations on street parties, with families decking out their houses in bunting and toasting the Greatest Generation from their doorstep or front garden. In Cannock, Staffordshire, twelve-year-old CJ Lloyd bought 100 Union flags with the pocket money he had saved for three weeks. 'We have been and given the flags to our neighbours and they have said how happy it has made them already,' CJ's mum told the local paper.

* * *

Deep in the forests of the Morvan during the summer of 1944, Captain Fraser McLuskey conducted church services in the hope he might be able to impart some of the Bible's teachings to the men. He was sceptical as to what the soldiers took on board. They stood before the padre not out of faith, but out of fellowship.

'Many of these men were living their lives outside the fellowship and discipline of Christian worship,' wrote Fraser. 'I thought of individual men among the officers, the NCOs and the men who had proved their courage and their skill in the strange new world of war; men who had given me so quickly and so freely their trust and their friendship. Pride in that gift has not lessened; I suppose there is nothing I value more . . . it was easy to be brave in their company and difficult to be a coward. I know that I shall never wholly lose the infection of their courage and good cheer.'

This was the same 'spiritual wealth' of which Tom Winter talked about in London during the Blitz. As our response to COVID-19 showed, it remains among Brits – at least most of us who don't waste our time in the vain and inane world of Twitter.

3

Ingenuity

There is a picture on my wall that was painted by Mike Carr. It's no masterpiece but I liked it the moment I saw it. That was in 2014 when I visited Mike at his home in the north-west of England to talk about his wartime service in the Long Range Desert Group.

The picture is of a spider's web, painted with small, delicate brush strokes. It was its ingenuity that caught my eye when I saw it on Mike's wall. He gave me the painting when I left, and I treasure it as the memento of a remarkable man.

Mike – or 'Lofty' as his pals in the LRDG called him on account of his 6ft 5in stature – was born in Somerset in 1920 to a working-class family. His grandfather was an army bandmaster and, on leaving the military, he worked as a steward on passenger ships between Britain and

Australia. Astronomy became a hobby of his as he voyaged back and forth across the globe, and his grandson inherited his passion. For his thirteenth birthday, Mike received from his grandfather a theodolite and a book about star charts and so began his interest in stars and navigation.

As Mike got to grips with his gift, thousands of miles away, another theodolite was in the deft hands of Ralph Bagnold. A veteran of the First World War, Bagnold was posted to Egypt in the 1920s and became fascinated by the Western Desert. With a small band of other intrepid army officers, Bagnold explored the desert in a Model T Ford in a series of adventures from 1927–33, penetrating its unforgiving interior as no other European had done.

Despite being born at the tail end of the Victorian era, Bagnold was a very modern thinker and his inventive mind was intrigued by what it encountered in the desert. On leaving the army in 1935, he wrote a book – *The Physics of Blown Sand and Desert Dunes* – and his expertise on the subject was in demand on both sides of the Atlantic.

Mike met Bagnold for the first time in January 1941 in Cairo. The war had uprooted both and brought them together. At first glance, they had little in common – twenty-four years separated them in age and there was a similar gulf in social class.

What created a bond was their inquisitive minds. Bagnold had devised an idea for a small reconnaissance force to head deep into the Libyan desert and gather intelligence on the disposition of Italian forces. Twice his proposal was rejected by senior officers unable to understand how inter-war advances in transport and communications had ushered in a new form of warfare. Only in June 1940, when Italy declared war on Britain, did Bagnold receive authorisation to put his innovation into practice.

Bagnold was given just six weeks to raise his unit, which was called the Long Range Desert Group (LRDG), but he accomplished the feat with astounding rapidity. Most of his officers were his explorer friends from pre-war days, and the other ranks were New Zealanders recruited by Bagnold because he considered Kiwis the most resourceful and ingenious of Commonwealth troops.

Bagnold kitted out their vehicles – American Chevrolet trucks – with the gadgets he'd invented in his exploration days. One such invention was his water condenser, consisting of two-gallon cans bolted to the running board of vehicles with a rubber tube leading to the radiator, so that when the water in the radiator boiled, the steam condensed in the can, and when it had stopped boiling the vacuum in the radiator would suck the water back and fill it up again.

There were also the sun compasses, a knitting needle set vertically in the centre of a horizontal white shadow disc, 3in in diameter. The face of the disc was graduated in 360 degrees of bearing, and the disc could be rotated in its fixed mounting to follow the sun through the day from east through south to west, according to a card giving the sun's azimuth every ten minutes of the day.

And there were also sand channels, a simple but ingenious method of extracting a vehicle from deep sand, by positioning a long steel panel in front of the rear wheels so that they could bite as the car accelerated forward.

'Bagnold was an ideas man, they came off his bat the whole time,' Mike told me. Mike was recruited into the LRDG in January 1941 when Bagnold expanded the group and put out a call for expert navigators. There were few to be found in the British Army. Mike was one, and his talents were being sorely wasted in the Staffordshire Yeomanry. He was bored in this regiment and from his ennui grew a truculence that made Mike's commanding officer only too happy to offload him into the LRDG.

There Mike found his calling. The LRDG welcomed disciplined outsiders, men of creativity and unorthodoxy who found regular soldiering stultifying. In Bagnold, Mike found a mentor, the man who would shape his life.

They spent hours talking on long road trips between Cairo and Kharga, 350 miles south of the Egyptian capital, when Mike would drive Bagnold for meetings with tribal headsmen. The older man passed on his experience to his protégé. 'Bagnold always said that when faced with a problem, you start by discarding the first three solutions, and then you start thinking of ways to solve the problem,' reflected Mike. 'You do that because the first three solutions will always be anticipated but not those when you think hard.'

Even in a unit as highly skilled as the LRDG, Mike became one of the most proficient navigators. David Stirling, the founder of the SAS, tried to headhunt him not long after he established his unit but Mike's loyalty was with the LRDG; they were the brains to the SAS brawn, in his opinion. In fact, the SAS had their own brains trust, notably Jock Lewes, whose eponymous bomb – a lump of plastic explosive and thermite rolled in motor car oil with a detonator, instantaneous fuse and a time pencil – was as ingenious as it was destructive when placed on an enemy aircraft.

Mike's war ended in September 1942 when he was captured during an attack on an enemy fort and he didn't return home until the spring of 1945.

By then, the LRDG was the most famous special forces unit in Britain. At a lecture to the Royal Geographical Society in January 1945, Bagnold explained the reason for their success. The right equipment and organisation was, of course, of paramount importance, as was secrecy, but it was the 'human element' that mattered most. 'We had to have tough and self-reliant volunteers, but they had to be highly intelligent men, too, capable of quick adaption to entirely new ways of life,' explained Bagnold.

* * *

The Greatest Generation displayed many virtues during the war, but perhaps none was as admirable as the alacrity with which they adapted to new circumstances, which, in turn, was made possible by their ingenuity. Necessity is the mother of invention and its offspring were multitudinous throughout the Second World War, not just on the battlefield or at Bletchley Park – where Alan Turing and the other codebreakers made such an important contribution – but on the home front and in prison camps, where ingenuity was required not to help win battles but to sustain hope in the most wretched of situations.

Langdon Gilkey, a twenty-four-year-old American, was teaching English in China when the Japanese invaded and he was interned in Shantung Compound, spending two years as a prisoner with many other Westerners, including a large number of Britons. They represented a broad cross-section of society: teachers, merchants, office workers, aid workers and prostitutes. Gilkey witnessed the gamut of human nature in the camp, some of it uplifting and some of it dispiriting; what also struck him was the 'inventiveness' of people who, for the most part, had led humdrum and unchallenging lives prior to their incarceration. 'However strange the world in which they may be set down, they will adapt themselves to it bravely,' he wrote of his fellow prisoners. 'Then gradually their ingenuity will find means to improve their situation. No problem of sanitation, cooking or drama was so difficult that some means can not be devised to cope with it.'

Gilkey and the other 2,000 prisoners in the Shantung Compound had a comparatively benign environment in which to cultivate their ingenuity. That wasn't the case for the Allied soldiers captured by the Japanese. To surrender was dishonourable in the eyes of the Japanese, and the British, Australian and American prisoners were subjected to the most degrading treatment imaginable. Yet out of the inhumanity grew inventiveness, nourishing the prisoners and allowing them to retain some semblance of dignity.

Colonel Cary Owtram was the British camp commandant at Chungkai from where Allied POWs were put to work on building the Burma to Thailand railway. Between June 1942 and October 1943, the POWs and forced labourers laid 258 miles (415km) of track, often slaving eighteen hours a day with little food, riddled with disease and routinely beaten by sadistic guards.

Yet when Owtram celebrated his forty-fourth birthday on 8 September 1943, he was presented with a birthday card, beefsteak pie, a birthday cake and a beer made from fermented rice, sugar and other ingredients to which he wasn't privy. 'By ingenuity, resource and a good deal of self-sacrifice on the part of kindly people, there were occasions upon which truly wonderful culinary efforts were produced,' he wrote.

This ingenuity stretched to far more than just a birthday party. The prisoners staged a Chungkai Derby with 'horses' made of painted boards that 'progressed uncertainly over a hazardous course according to the throws of a huge wooden dice'. There was even a tote and stakes won and lost.

Prisoners made a football and an international league was formed, with the winning nation being presented with a shield fashioned from wooden boxes. Owtram described it as 'a work of art'.

Medical staff improvised saline injections to treat a cholera outbreak using water distilled in four-gallon petrol tins over a wood fire, and a physical training instructor established a Remedial Centre in which prisoners who had lost the use of their limbs for one reason or another were coaxed back to mobility with the aid of a gentle rehabilitation programme.

Prisoners grew their own vegetables such as maize, French beans and sweet potatoes. Owtram was particularly proud of his tomatoes, which 'would have done credit to a market gardener anywhere'.

But the greatest ingenuity was seen in the camp concerts. 'We started with very humble and amateurish entertainments,' wrote Owtram, 'but once given opportunity . . . we had a complete theatre with drop curtains, footlights, dressing rooms, wardrobe masters.'

The pride and joy was the orchestra, which consisted of a bugle, homemade bass drum and a cello and violin made out of fish boxes and some local hardwood with telephone wire for the strings. The camp concert party was a chance not just for prisoners to laugh and sing, but to take pride in their ingenuity.

* * *

Britons on the home front also endured a form of imprisonment during the war. Marooned on their island with German U-boats sinking the ships that brought provisions from overseas (in 1939, about 60 per cent of Britain's food was imported), men and particularly women and children had to be ingenious to compensate for the shortages. Food was the gravest challenge but the lack of textiles and cosmetics caused angst among the more fashion-conscious.

Una Quibell, a twenty-one-year-old munitions worker in Middlesex, recalled using parsnips, beetroot and carrots to sweeten cakes and buns to replace the dearth of dried fruits. She grew vegetables on top of the Anderson shelter in her backyard (as did many others), but she couldn't bring herself to imitate the many women of her generation who stained their legs with cold tea or gravy browning because there were no stockings to be had in the shops. Una believed it was better to be bare-legged than smell of a Sunday roast. Some women overcame the shortage of lipstick by applying beetroot juice.

Heather Woodley's family also grew their own vegetables (in total, ten million acres of grassland were dug up for vegetable growing as part of the 'Dig for Victory' campaign, and consequently Britain's dependence on imported foods dropped to one-third of its population's needs). Of her mother's ingenuity in the kitchen, Heather reflected, 'She tried hard to make meals that were appetising and she became an expert, as did many other mums, at making ends meet with what little she had. One of my favourites was bacon and onion pudding, which used a small amount of bacon rolled with sliced onions and steamed in a suet pastry. This made a nourishing and filling meal for the family. Ingenious ways of preparing food were invented to try to make food taste palatable. To mimic the flavour and texture of bananas, parsnips were boiled until softened, then mashed and banana essence mixed into it. Ice cream was made of soya or rice pudding.'

One of my dad's earliest memories is helping his mother grow vegetables in their small back garden to feed them and the two RAF personnel from a nearby Wellington bomber airfield billeted with them. He's still growing vegetables eighty-two years later.

* * *

In its edition of 19 July 1940, the *Dover Express* declared that 'women are discovering that economy is a virtue, which earns more than its own reward. The simple wartime diet as recommended by the Ministry of Food is earning dividends in the form of slim waists and good complexions . . . a "milkmaid complexion" and sylph-figure will be legacies of the war.'

The 'sylph-figures' were frequently forced into outfits that were more practical than elegant, but spending every night in a cold, damp air-raid shelter had a tendency to make even the most dedicated follower of fashion lose their way. Siren Suits (shamelessly ripped off by today's onesies!) were designed to be slipped over one's clothes the moment the air-raid siren sounded. Harrods, Jaeger and Harvey Nichols sold their own, but most people fashioned theirs using guides published in magazines.

When rationing and clothing coupons didn't stretch to a new dress, women made their own from curtains and bedspreads. 'Make Do and Mend' became one of the most famous slogans of the war and, if mothers were occupied cooking and sewing, their children were doing their bit for the war effort by recycling, collecting empty cigarette cartons, cleaning powder and cereal packing for official collection, along with more exciting items.

'Collecting cartridges, cannon shell cases, anti-aircraft shells and shrapnel with incendiary bomb fins was quite an industry with us children,' recalled Peter Brewer. 'Picking up those items, particularly the cases, was hazardous and sometimes they were still hot. It was collected at centres for eventual conversion to Spitfire manufacture.'

The war for many children was a time of excitement, almost of liberation, certainly for the Londoners who wrote to me with their memories. 'I was old enough to be excited and thrilled by what was going on but young enough not to be really scared,' reflected Peter, who was born in 1930. 'I, in company with many youngsters, appreciated the disrupted schooling! We spent months living at night in the Anderson air-raid shelter. One could set one's watch by the regularity of the Luftwaffe's nightly appearance.'

Families took board games and packs of cards into their shelters, but most of all they took books. Publishers saw a niche and, during the first winter of the war, a slew of titles were published with ideas for passing the night in the shelter. One of the most popular was *The Black-Out Book*, a compendium of puzzles, magic tricks, spelling bees, quizzes and games. The book began with a quote from GK Chesterton: 'Of all modern notions, the worst is this: that domesticity is dull . . . the home is not the one tame place in a world of adventure; it is the one wild place in a world of rules and set tasks.'

Anderson shelters, which were 6ft in height and length and 4ft 6in wide, became a cradle of creativity, a microcosm of the country as a whole during the six years of the Second World War.

* * *

Ingenuity isn't a trait like stoicism or selflessness; it's not innate or instilled in our formative years. It's often born from necessity, as Langdon Gilkey noted when describing the inspiring inventiveness he witnessed in the Shantung Compound. 'However strange the world in which they may be set down, they will adapt themselves to it bravely,' he wrote. 'Then gradually their ingenuity will find means to improve their situation.'

This was true during the lockdown in Britain – for some. A nation that had lived orderly and organised lives suddenly had to improvise – whether eating, exercising, working or enjoying leisure time. The retailer John Lewis reported an unprecedented demand for haberdashery items with sales of elastic rocketing 1,430 per cent as people made their own face masks.

There were many reports of schools across Britain putting their technology departments to good use to produce face masks. At Mearns Castle High School in Scotland, a laser-cutter was used to make visors for NHS staff and, in Bath, Prior Park College made 500 visors in three days. 'The feedback has been overwhelming!' said one of the teachers. 'I personally have taken phone calls for support from all around the country and have shared the cutting files and designs with companies in Kent, Manchester and even America!'

In Waterlooville, fifty-nine-year-old John Harris worked round the clock to produce 600 visors for medical staff on his three 3D printers. 'Nurses cherish them,' John said. 'The ones they were wearing before were big and cumbersome, whereas these are lightweight and much more comfortable, as well as being solid, too.'

There was creativity, too, in our culinary habits, with supermarket Waitrose reporting a huge spike in sales of pasta machines, bakeware and food processors. 'While we've been in lockdown, our focus has shifted on to making the most of our store cupboards and freezers, while coming up with inspiring and varied dishes to see us through,' remarked Alison Oakervee, the food editor at Waitrose.

Another supermarket, Tesco, reported that 20 per cent have used the lockdown to experiment in the kitchen, broadening their range of recipes, and 35 per cent admitted they now used leftovers to avoid food waste.

The *Guardian* asked its readers how they were keeping fit during the lockdown and there were many examples of ingenuity. One woman had manufactured a barbell from a couple of beer casks cadged from her local pub and a length of bamboo; a man had built a climbing wall in his garage and another climbed the equivalent of Snowdon and Scafell Pike using his garden steps, having calculated the number of repetitions required to scale the two peaks.

There was also a fecundity to fund-raising. Two NHS managers in Kent launched a Bake, Donate, Nominate campaign in which people baked a cake, donated a minimum £5 to their local NHS Trust and then nominated up to five friends to do the same via social media; and seven-year-old Issy Ashbullby raised money for the upkeep of the Axe Valley Animal Park in Kilmington by drawing twenty-six pictures of the animals at the park and inviting donations via the Internet.

We Brits have always prided ourselves on our ingenuity and among our most celebrated inventions are the television and the World Wide Web. Unfortunately in recent years, we've become too addicted to the twin screens.

A survey on digital literacy released in February 2020 by the DQ Institute, a think tank partnered with the World Economic Forum, found that British children aged 8–19 spent on average 44 hours a week staring at screens such as computers, mobile phones and television. Of the thirty countries analysed, only the Dominican Republic had a lower ranking for 'disciplined digital use' in the DQ Institute's report.

As the nation's digital dependency increases, its practical prowess decreases. A report in the *Daily Mirror* in 2017 found that 75 per cent of 18–35-year-olds didn't know how to fry an egg or boil vegetables and, in the same year, the British Heart Foundation reported that 60 per cent of the same age group didn't know how to sew and half of young Britons had to ask their mothers to help with mending.

Those who felt too embarrassed to lean on Mum 'spent an unnecessary £3 billion on replacement clothes last year, which could have been mended'. For the self-styled 'green' generation, such wastage should make Millennials red with embarrassment.

So let's hope that a legacy of the lockdown will be a broadening of creative horizons, whether it's using a crayon, cooking utensil, laser-cutter or needle and thread. It's never to late to invent a new life, as Mike Carr proved in the 1960s.

Mike went into insurance after the war. Then, one day in his mid-forties, he woke up and realised he was 'in a slow glide to the grave'. Call it a mid-life crisis. So he enrolled in an art course in his local college of education and spent the last twenty years of his working life teaching art to schoolchildren. 'There may be a message in this for some,' he wrote in a letter published in the LRDG journal of 1970. 'Let's start something rather than wait for the end.'

4

Liberality

The first wartime veteran of the SAS I met was Malcolm Pleydell. He had been their medical officer in North Africa throughout 1942 and, shortly after the war, he wrote his memoir, *Born of the Desert*, under the *nom de plume* Malcolm James. It remains, in my opinion, the definitive book about the wartime SAS.

Malcolm was very frail when I visited him in 1998, but he signed my copy of the book and we talked for a while about those bygone days. I was particularly keen to hear Malcolm's view on Paddy Mayne, arguably the greatest guerrilla fighter of the Second World War – certainly the most lethal.

In *Born of the Desert*, Malcolm recalled Paddy setting off on an operation in the hope there would be some 'good killing'. Paddy enjoyed war, enjoyed danger and, having interviewed many men who fought with him, enjoyed killing. 'Paddy was a bit different from the others,' wrote Malcolm. 'This sort of fighting was in his blood; he thrived on it. There was no give or take about his method of warfare, and he was out to kill when the opportunity presented itself.'

For a man whose duty it was to preserve life, one might have expected Malcolm and Paddy to have had little in common; in fact, they were friends, sharing a love of literature, history and nature. They were also both liberals.

In recent years, Paddy has been described in the media as a 'social misfit' or a 'psychopath', a predictable, narrow-minded assessment in an age when, increasingly, humans can only be 'villains' or 'virtuous'. Like all of us, Paddy was complex. On the one hand a killer, and on the other a lover of arts.

He was a graduate of Queen's University, a qualified solicitor and an international rugby player, a man of eclectic cultural tastes. He was a Protestant from Northern Ireland but, recalled Malcolm, he selected several men from the Republic of Ireland for his squadron in the autumn of 1942. 'They all had shamrocks painted on their jeeps and I know he was proud of them.'

Paddy assumed command of the SAS in early 1943 after the capture of David Stirling. It was a transformative period. The war in the desert was nearing its climax and the SAS was undergoing a period of restructuring and retraining in expectation of operations in southern Europe. They were also recruiting and among the volunteers who arrived at their camp was Keith Killby.

Keith was a man of strong convictions yet physically one of the gentlest veterans I've met. He died in 2018 in his 103rd year. I met him fifteen years earlier when he told me about his encounter with Paddy Mayne.

Keith was a Londoner, from a family involved in the meat trade. In his youth, he became a pacifist but, on the outbreak of war, he enlisted as a conscientious objector in the Royal Army Medical Corps (RAMC). He served in North Africa with the 150th Field Ambulance Unit attached to the 50th Division and, in May 1942, his commanding officer, Lieutenant Colonel William Scriven, praised Keith's 'courage and devotion to duty in assisting with the treatment of German wounded under shellfire'.

In late 1942, Keith fell ill with jaundice and, on recovering, he was sent to the RAMC depot. An acquaintance told him about a unit looking for medical orderlies – the SAS. Apparently, so Keith was told, the initials stood for 'Special Ambulance Service' and, what was more, they paid an additional sixpence a day.

Keith volunteered and, a few days later, arrived at their camp in Kabrit, east of Cairo. The first thing that struck him was the 'unorthodoxy' of the SAS uniform. When he learned that SAS didn't stand for 'Special Ambulance Service' he thought, 'Well, they won't want me.'

All the same, he was told to report to Paddy's tent. Keith's first job was to bandage the hands Paddy had bruised the previous evening in a Cairo brawl. He asked about Keith's military experience. Keith told him, then blurted out nervously, 'Sir, you know I'm a conscientious objector?'

In his soft voice, Paddy asked why. Was it to do with religion? No, replied Keith, and explained that it was a long-standing pacifism. Paddy had no problem with that. Keith had proved he was cool under fire, a man of moral and physical courage. Keith was offered a role in the SAS.

Keith would soon discover that he was the latest in a long line of diverse recruits to the SAS. For instance there was a young homosexual officer called Bill Fraser; an ardent communist in Arthur Phillips; an American by the name of Pat Riley; Charles Bonington, the son of a German merchant seaman; Karl Kahane, an Austrian Jew and former regular in the German army, Dave Kershaw, who had fought for the Republicans in the Spanish Civil War; and Jock Lewes, a right-wing Oxford graduate.

They were all accepted. What mattered to their leader, David Stirling, wasn't their background but their courage, competency and character.

Stirling was no doubt influenced by his family's experience a quarter of a century earlier. In 1910, his father, then Captain Archibald Stirling, had married the Honourable Margaret Lovat, converting to her Catholic faith in order to win her hand. He was never forgiven by many in Scotland. When Stirling (by now a general) contested the 1918 General Election as the Unionist Coalition candidate for Kinross and West Perthshire, he lost. The people, explained the local paper, were not prepared to vote for 'a papist'.

David Stirling grew up a liberal and, like many of his generation, despised the bigotry of his elders, many of whom held positions of seniority in the British Army at the time he was forming the SAS. 'Fossilised shits,' he called them, a view endorsed by his men.

* * *

One of the most odious calumnies perpetuated by opponents of Brexit was that the Leave vote was the fault of old people, and that the sooner these intolerant 'Gammons' died the better, so that Britain could remain in the European Union. The novelist Ian McEwan generalised Brexit voters as 'a gang of angry old men, irritable even in victory, (who) are shaping the future of the country against the inclinations of its youth'. The editor of the *New European*, Matt Kelly, tweeted a photo of the audience attending a Brexit Party event with the caption: 'Marvel at the diversity, behold the spread of demographics. And bring a mop to clear up the leaked piss afterwards.'

The broadcaster Terry Christian wished for 'a good virulent strain' of 'flu to kill off the old people who had 'voted to destroy our lives'.

I discussed Brexit with two special forces veterans of the Second World War – one voted Leave and the other Remain, the latter doing so for the sake of his grandchildren. He wasn't alone. Prior to the 2016 referendum, several veterans threw their support behind the Remain vote, notably Field Marshal Bramall, who took part in the D-Day landings and subsequently became Chief of the Defence Staff.

Britain, once upon a time, was the world leader in liberality. Arguably, its apogee was in the late 1930s when approximately 10,000 Jewish children from Germany, Austria, Poland and Czechoslovakia arrived in the UK. They were taken in by foster parents, who had responded to a public appeal from a young charity worker, Nicholas Winton, to 'help to save the children of this courageous and desperately unfortunate people'.

Once war was declared, thousands of young men and women arrived from countries then under the yoke of the Nazis, including Poland, Czechoslovakia, Belgium and France. All were made welcome, except for a few Frenchmen whose Anglophobia angered their hosts. That's always been the British way – everyone welcome as long as you pull your weight.

One man who pulled his weight was Ronald Grierson – or, as he was called on his birth certificate, Rolf Hans Griessman. Born in Nuremberg in 1921, young Rolf and his Jewish family fled Germany shortly after Hitler came to power. He was educated in London and changed his name to 'Grierson' in 1943, choosing the name from a telephone directory.

When I interviewed Sir Ronald, as he then was, in 2002 at his Pall Mall office, he was one of Britain's richest and most respected bankers, industrialists and public servants. I was there to discuss his service with the SAS in 1944–45. Had he faced any hostility when he joined the regiment? I asked. None, he replied. He was welcomed as just another soldier.

I recall asking a similar question of several SAS veterans about Bill Fraser, the homosexual officer. 'It was obvious he was queer,' one told me. 'But we didn't care. He was a bloody good officer.'

In the Desert War, the SAS, and more particularly the LRDG, frequently came into contact with the Senussi, an indigenous people of the Libyan desert. The Italians butchered them; the British learned from them. Ralph Bagnold, the founder of the LRDG and a man who had first explored the Libyan desert in the 1920s, would often meet with the people's leaders to pick their brains. One of Bagnold's chief navigators, Mike 'Lofty' Carr, was once sheltered by a Senussi clan for a week after becoming separated from his patrol. 'They are a strict sect and I know Bagnold had huge respect for them,' he told me. 'We all did. They are such a dignified people, pure and highly refined.'

Mike told me another story about one of their fitters (mechanics), Scotty, who was an Anglo-Indian and one of the LRDG's most skilled technicians. One day another soldier – Mike called him 'Shithouse' – racially and physically abused Scotty. 'So we hoofed him off,' said Mike. 'We didn't want people like that in the LRDG.'

Incidentally, I have in my possession the 1969 edition of the LRDG Association journal in which there is a letter from a wartime member of the unit, Bryn Pritchard. He recounted an incident after the 1968 LRDG reunion in central London as he waited for a Tube train at Euston. 'A young twerp was being very offensive to a number of coloured people who were taking as little notice as possible,' wrote Bryn. 'The language was definitely foul and trouble-making so I suggested a good rinse with soap and water.'

The yob persisted in hurling racial abuse so Bryn 'was forced to chastise him with a good smack on the mouth'. A second lout weighed in, slashing Bryn's nose with a shard of glass, but he fought his way out of the situation and on to a train. 'All the same, I had enjoyed the reunion,' he concluded his letter. 'Stripper and all.'

The Greatest Generation were certainly liberal when it came to the opposite sex. As one SAS veteran confided to me, 'The best thing about the war was I got to sleep with lots of girls from different countries.' Norwegians were a particular favourite. When the SAS were stationed in Bergen in the summer of 1945, they came to blows on several occasions with young local men who wanted to punish women for fraternising with Germans during the Occupation; the SAS had been appalled at some of the treatment meted out to Frenchwomen after the liberation and they vowed there would be no repeat in Norway. The antagonism between the local 'tough guys' and the SAS culminated in what came to be known as the 'Battle of Bergen'; in truth, it wasn't much of a battle. The Norwegians were roundly thrashed. To celebrate their victory, the SAS threw a ball, and advertised it with a poster in their billet: 'Bring your own collaborator'.

Like Keith Killby, the author Vera Brittain was a pacifist, the result of her experience in the First World War when she lost her brother, fiancé and two best friends in the trenches. She was a keen observer in May 1940 of the trial of six members of the Peace Pledge Union, Christian pacifists who were in the dock to answer charges of acting against the interest of Britain. Their 'crime' was the exhibition of a poster displaying the words: 'War will cease when men refuse to fight. What are YOU going to do about it?'

Some of the newspapers wanted them jailed. The *Sunday Mirror* described the six as 'conchies' and 'rats', but the magistrate, Mr Justice Stable, threw out the charge, stating in his summing up, 'This is a free country. We are fighting to keep it a free country, as I understand it, and these gentlemen, fortunately for them, in my judgement, are living in a country where they can express their pacifism, or their non-pacifism, with perfect freedom.'

Vera Brittain was proud and delighted by the verdict, writing: 'It establishes the principle, later embodied in a Memorandum issued by the Home Secretary (Sir John Anderson) on 26 July 1940, that "in this country no person should be penalised for the mere holding of an opinion, however unpopular that opinion may be to the majority"'.

Winston Churchill had exhibited similar tolerance the previous March after the BBC banned several figures from the art world from appearing on the airwaves. The Beeb's beef was that they had expressed sympathy for the 'People's Convention', a coalition of communists, trade unionists and pacifists that held its inaugural rally in January 1941. Numerous speakers among the 2,300 delegates present in London had questioned Britain's involvement in a war that would be of little benefit to the workers.

Churchill believed it unjust to deny artists a platform on which to perform because of their political views and he pressurised the BBC to rescind the ban, which they did.

He also asked them to reinstate two technicians who had been dismissed for their pacifism. 'The rights which have been granted in this war, and in the last, to conscientious objectors are well known,' Churchill told Parliament, 'and are a definite part of British policy. Anything in the nature of persecution, victimisation or manhunting is odious to the British people.'

Were that still the case. But a sinister wave of illiberalism is sweeping Britain, endangering free speech to such an extent that a High Court in 2020 likened Humberside Police to the 'Gestapo' because of their attempt to stifle the freedom of expression of a man who 'liked' a tweet questioning transgender people.

Two months earlier, a woman lost her appeal against dismissal for tweeting that transgender women cannot change their biological sex. Judge James Tayler called the woman an 'absolutist' for her views that he described as 'intimidating, hostile, degrading, humiliating or offensive . . . not worthy of respect in a democratic society'.

Too numerous to mention are the men and women who have had their livelihoods undermined for one ideological crime or another. Dozens of writers, thinkers and campaigners from a broad cross-section of society have been 'no-platformed' by universities, simply for being ideologically out of step with the new and very narrow dogma, and barely a week goes by without a social media mob chasing after some unfortunate for a remark judged unacceptable. JK Rowling is a particular target for the new intolerants; in the summer of 2020, four authors quit the literary agency they shared with the Harry Potter creator after she implied that only women could menstruate. 'Freedom of speech can only be upheld if the structural inequalities that hinder equal opportunities for under-represented groups are challenged and changed,' said the quartet in a statement announcing their decision. That act was probably a contributory factor to the publication in July in *Harper*'s magazine of a letter signed by 150 writers and academics – among them Rowling, Noam Chomsky, Salman Rushdie and Margaret Atwood – in which they warned that 'the free exchange of information and ideas, the lifeblood of a liberal society, is daily becoming more constricted'.

A new illiberal craze took hold during the lockdown when ideological tyrants scrutinised the bookshelves of interviewees as they talked to the camera. Michael Gove, for example, was criticised in some quarters when it was spotted that among the biographies of Mussolini, Stalin, Thatcher and Napoleon was a book written by David Irving, the Holocaust denier. This apparently made him a Nazi. Stephen Pollard, the editor of the *Jewish Chronicle*, called the furore 'deranged', adding, 'If that's how it works, I am beyond redemption. As well as two books by Irving,

I've got a book by the actual Adolf Hitler on my shelves, not to mention Mao.'

Talking of Chairman Mao, he appears to be the inspiration for a growing number of young Britons who, during the lockdown, embarked on their own Cultural Revolution. Anyone who dared challenge their desire to rewrite Britain's history was aggressively told to 'educate themselves'. That was the purpose of the re-education camps set up by Mao in the 1950s in which thousands of thinkers, writers, doctors and teachers were taught the error of their ideological ways.

Held in particular contempt by Britain's 'Red Guard' is the generation whose opinions are rejected with a sneering 'OK, Boomer'. A couple of Baby-Boomers had their collars felt by the Thought Police during the lockdown for challenging its validity – the columnist Peter Hitchens and the retired Justice of the Supreme Court Jonathan Sumption. They were among the small minority of commentators who opposed the lockdown from the start because they viewed it as ineffective and illiberal. Sumption, in particular, was eloquent about what he regarded as the hysterical over-reaction to COVID-19. 'We have acquired an irrational horror of death,' he said. 'In the midst of life, our ancestors lived with death, an ever-present fact that they understood.'

A columnist in the *Guardian* labelled Sumption 'bizarre' for his 'open indifference to other people's agony', which was a twisting of his words. But that is a typical tactic of the new illiberals – to shame the dissenters into silence. Either that, or simply censor them, as YouTube did during the COVID-19 pandemic, removing videos from its website (including interviews from Peter Hitchens and Professor Karol Sikora) because they deviated from the lockdown orthodoxy.

There was censorship in Britain during the war, of course, but that was imposed by a Government fighting a tangible enemy; the purpose of the new censorship is to silence any dissenting voice. The famous wartime slogan in Britain of 'Careless Talk Costs Lives' could be reworked in 2020 to read 'Careless Talk Costs Livelihoods'. It's not enemy spies who are the danger, it's illiberals.

There are signs that the British people have had enough and wish to return to the liberality championed in 1940 by Sir John Anderson, who declared that 'no person should be penalised for the mere holding of an opinion, however unpopular that opinion may be to the majority'.

A Free Speech Union was launched in 2019 and, in 2020, the Campaign for Common Sense (CCS) was established, which described itself 'as a rallying point for people who have had enough of walking on eggshells'. On the day it launched, the CCS released a survey that revealed 84 per cent of people polled agreed with the statement: 'We need to restore some common sense in this country.' 61 per cent agreed that political correctness endows 'too much power to a small minority of people who like to take offence'.

These people have always been around. In 1940, George Orwell wrote that what marked them out was their 'generally negative, querulous attitude, their complete lack at all times of any constructive suggestion (and) there is little in them except the irresponsible carping of people who have never been and never expect to be in a position of power'.

But now their grandchildren are in positions of power and, furthermore, social media is the perfect platform from which to wield that power, as YouTube demonstrated.

They like to think of themselves as liberal and tolerant, accepting of all colours and creeds, but they are utterly intolerant of anyone who diverges from their narrow thinking. In 1940, Orwell wrote that despite the war, and the millions of men and women being called up to perform various duties, the British were at heart libertarians. 'The English are in process of being numbered, labelled, conscripted, co-ordinated,' he wrote. 'But the pull of their impulses is in the other direction, and the kind of regimentation that can be imposed on them will be modified in consequence. No party rallies, no Youth Movements, no coloured shirts, no Jew-baiting or "spontaneous" demonstrations. No Gestapo either, in all probability.'

Does that still ring true? In 2020, the British were conscripted into an indefinite lockdown and the minority of dissenters were labelled as 'covidiots'. Twitter, at times, feels like a giant party rally and anyone with a view that is contrary to the majority is demonised.

It's time for true liberals to push back against the creeping tide of intolerance in Britain, as they did during the Second World War. To mark the dawn of 1941, Harvard and Yale sent messages of greeting to the Vice-Chancellors of Oxford and Cambridge in which they praised their defence of intellectual freedom at a time of national peril. In their response, the Vice-Chancellors vowed 'to maintain the continuity of scholarship and to keep, even in these days, the standards of knowledge unimpaired and the sources of truth unsoiled.'

The Vice-Chancellor of Oxford also sent a message of solidarity to the University of Paris, and envisaged a day when intellectual liberty would return. In reporting the exchange of messages between what it called the 'famous sanctuaries of humane culture', *The Times* in its leader of 9 January 1941 commented: 'More menacing to the values for which we fight than anything inherent in the mere forms of government is this claim of Nazism to suppress the spirit of free inquiry and to impose its own party doctrines as unquestionable truth; and all safeguards for peace . . . will fail if it is ever again possible for a Government to draw an intellectual frontier round its subjects and cut them off from contact with the thought of the world.'

Keith Killby shared this dislike of frontiers. 'When I was at school, I heard a story about a pudding that took 1,000 hands to make,' he told me. 'It showed how the pudding basin was made in Czechoslovakia, the raisins came from Australia, the flour from Canada, etc., etc., . . . and it sort of gave me the idea that the world was one.'

This was the story Keith told to Paddy Mayne when asked to account for his pacifism. Mayne was a killer, arguably the most effective of his generation of British soldiers, but he was also liberal-minded, a defender of intellectual freedom, just as much as the Vice-Chancellors of Oxford and Cambridge.

5

Selflessness

When I visited Gladys Shaw in April 2004, she had baked a cake for the occasion. She had her best tableware out, too, and over tea and cake we talked. I was researching a book about the Blitz and Gladys had responded to an advert I'd placed in a magazine. She was in her 93rd year, a small demure woman whose home in Sussex reflected its owner's character.

Gladys was born into a middle-class family in 1911; her father was a journalist for a newspaper in Brighton but, in 1936, the year that George Orwell wrote *The Road to Wigan Pier*, Gladys joined the Ranyard Mission, formerly known as the Bible and Domestic Female Mission. Mr Shaw was aghast. His religion had been knocked out of him on the Western Front in 1916.

At the end of her first day among the most desperate slums of south London, Gladys wept at the misery she had witnessed. It took several months for Gladys to be accepted by the people of Peckham. Some, at first, were suspicious of the young, middle-class woman, others resentful, and a few hostile.

Gladys giggled as she told me about some of the characters she encountered. Religious, they weren't. Petty crime and illegitimacy were rife yet there was also, she explained, an honesty to them. There were no airs and graces. What you saw what was you got. When she was invited into one home and given a cup of tea, she knew she'd been accepted.

When war broke out, Gladys remained in Peckham. As well as maintaining her missionary work, she signed up to work two nights a week at a first-aid post and another two as a firewatcher. Those nights weren't too bad because she was part of a team; the evenings she dreaded were the ones when she cycled through Peckham to comfort the people cowering in air-raid shelters. 'It was having to go out in a raid on one's own that was bad,' she told me. 'I always wished I had someone with me.'

On the evening of 10 May 1941, there was a hope that the Blitz was all but over. There hadn't been a raid for more than a fortnight and Londoners were daring to believe that Hitler had given up trying to demoralise them. But the Luftwaffe returned on this evening for a valedictory raid, a deadly farewell before they switched their focus to the imminent invasion of Russia.

The first bombs began dropping on the capital at 11.00pm and, by the time the last explosives fell at around 4.30am, 1,436 people had been killed, 1,800 wounded and 12,374 people had been left homeless.

Throughout those terrifying few hours, Gladys cycled from one street shelter to the next, pedalling furiously, one eye on the road, one on the bright moonlit sky, praying to her God. 'They loved it when I arrived,' recalled Gladys of the greeting she received from the frightened people inside the shelters. 'It made them feel protected when I read from the Bible, as if they were receiving God's blessing.'

Gladys spent a few minutes inside each shelter, as much for her own comfort as for the others. 'I knew that when I stepped out on to the street I would be on my own,' she said. 'It was only seven or eight minutes at the most between shelters but that feels like an awfully long time when you're dodging bombs alone.'

One bomb blew Gladys off her bicycle as she approached the Elephant & Castle. She scrambled behind a wall trembling with fear. Up ahead was a railway arch, but she didn't think she could summon up the courage to run to it. 'Suddenly I regained my composure,' she said. '"Don't be such a fool!" I remember saying to myself. I got to my feet and ran under the arch as fast as I could until I reached the next shelter.

I went in and someone said, "Hey, look at her, looking so cheerful on a dreadful night like this!" If I looked cheerful, I didn't feel it, but I'd beaten my fear.'

A year after the war ended, Gladys volunteered to go to rural India, where she spent thirty years as a missionary in some of the country's poorest regions. She retired in 1976 and returned to Sussex, where she lived until her death in 2013. 'Dearly loved sister, aunt, great-aunt and great-great-aunt, friend to so many both in England and India where she worked for many years,' ran her obituary. 'Gladys gave her body for medical science.'

Gladys' selflessness was exceptional, not only because of its longevity but also because during the Blitz she endangered her own life to bring succour to others.

Hers was a rare altruism. So, too, was Angus McGillivray's. He knew that his act of selflessness could have only one outcome but he never wavered from the course on which he set himself in a Japanese prisoner-of-war camp.

The twenty-seven-year-old was a private in the 2nd Battalion Argyll and Sutherland Highlanders when he was taken prisoner in Singapore in February 1942. Later that year, McGillivray and the rest of the Argylls were put to work on the Death Railway, the line the Japanese constructed through thick jungle to link Thailand to Burma. Conditions were inhumane. Tens of thousands of prisoners died of disease, exhaustion and malnutrition. Morale among the living plummeted. An 'every-man-for-himself' attitude began to spread. Prisoners even started to steal from one another. One particularly sick Argyll had his blanket stolen. His friend, or 'mucker', as the Argylls called their pals, was Angus McGillivray.

Angus saw the spirit drain from his mucker, so he gave him his own blanket. What happened next was recounted by Ernest Gordon in his book *Through the Valley of the Kwai*. 'Every mealtime, Angus would show up to draw his ration. But he didn't eat it. He would bring it round to give to his friend. Stood over him, he did, and made him eat it.'

Slowly McGillivray's 'mucker' improved, growing physically and psychologically stronger. All the while, McGillivray weakened until one day he 'just pitched on his face and died'. The camp doctor gave the cause of death as starvation and exhaustion. 'During the next few days, I heard other prisoners discussing Angus's sacrifice,' wrote Gordon. 'The story of what he had done was spreading through the camp. It had evidently fired the imagination of everyone. He had given us a shining example of the way we ought to live, even if we did not.'

McGillivray's sacrifice was remarkable because it was prolonged. It wasn't an instinctive act made in the heat of battle, like the soldier throwing himself on a grenade to protect his comrades. Both are vivid examples, nonetheless, of the passage in John that declares: 'Greater love hath no man than this, that he lay down his life for his friends.'

Flight-Lieutenant Harold Ken MacDonald gave his life for people he didn't know. In a dogfight with German Messerschmitts over Kent on 28 September 1940, MacDonald's Spitfire caught fire. 'He had been seen about to bale out of his blazing machine at 1,000ft,' wrote one of his fellow pilots in 603 Squadron, Richard Hillary. 'But as he was over a thickly populated area, he had climbed in again.' MacDonald, whose brother had been killed a fortnight earlier flying with the same squadron, piloted his burning aircraft away from the houses below and then baled out. But he was only 400 feet above ground, too low for his parachute to fully open.

Another 603 Squadron pilot killed in the bloody month of September 1940 was Flying Officer Peter Pease. He and Richard Hillary were best friends but intellectually and emotionally they were opposites. In his wartime memoir, *The Last Enemy*, published in 1942, Hillary recounted a conversation with Pease on a train from Montrose to Edinburgh in the summer of 1940. Hillary, a self-confessed 'selfish swine', wanted to know why Pease, a scion of a titled family and a product of Eton and Cambridge, was fighting the war. 'What I want is to see a better world come out of this war,' said Pease. 'I believe that we should all make our contribution, even though it's a mere drop in the ocean, to the betterment of humanity.'

Hillary sneered at Pease's Christian ideals and his ambition to enter politics after the war out of a misplaced sense of altruism, and told him, 'You are going to concern yourself with politics and mankind when the war is over; I am going to concern myself with the individual and Richard Hillary. I may or may not be exactly a man of my time, I don't know. But I know you are an anachronism.'

When Pease and MacDonald and many other of his fellow pilots were dead, Hillary, by now badly burned after being shot down, ruminated on that conversation in the train. 'Peter had been right,' he admitted. 'It was impossible to look only to oneself, to take from life and not to give except by accident, deliberately to look at humanity and then pass by on the other side. No longer could one say, "The world's my oyster and the hell with the rest."'

Hillary was killed on active service on 7 January 1943. His friend, Wing-Commander Doug Watkins, told the *Sunday Mirror* newspaper three days later that Hillary had been asked to write a script for an air-sea rescue film but he was 'desperately keen to get back flying, and I know he was delighted when he was passed medically fit'.

Another death that made the newspapers was that of Caleb Milne in May 1943. The *New York Times* reported that Milne had been killed in Tunisia serving as a medic with the American Field Service (AFS) attached to the British Eighth Army. The AFS comprised mainly conscientious objectors; many were intellectuals who had graduated from Harvard or Yale.

Milne's back story was different. In December 1935, he had faked his own kidnap in an attempt to extort $25,000 from his grandfather, a Pennsylvania textile tycoon. J Edgar Hoover and thirty of his FBI G-Men launched a manhunt and, after four days, Milne was found bound and gagged in a ditch about forty miles from Chester, Pennsylvania. Eventually, the twenty-four-year-old Milne admitted it was all a hoax 'inspired by need of money and by a belief that resultant publicity would help him get a job on the stage'.

Milne avoided prison but he was disinherited by his grandfather. He renounced his ambition to become an actor and studied architecture at university. He reassessed his life in much the same way Richard Hillary had done, and reached the same conclusion.

Milne's pacifism wasn't born from religion. Rather, as he told his mother in a letter on the eve of his departure to North Africa in June 1942, 'I am not foaming to bayonet anyone, nor am I embittered enough to throw precious life away for this momentary calamity that has spread like a disease over the world. I dream of the day when one may say, "I am a citizen of the world." I have never had a provincial sense to much degree, and it seems stupider and blinder than ever now to shout the old nationalistic battle hymns when they have brought the world into such artificial and complicated chaos.'

Milne was killed on 11 May 1943 in one of the last battles of the war in North Africa. A regiment of Free French had requested stretcher bearers from the AFS and Milne was among the twenty who had volunteered. He was killed as he tended the wounds of a French soldier.

Selflessness flourished on the home front as well as the battle front, much of it in small deeds unseen and unheralded. Kathleen Urry was nine when the Blitz started in London in 1940. 'One day, a few of us were on our way home from school when we heard planes coming over and, as there were no barrage balloons up, we thought the planes must be ours,' she told me. 'Then all of a sudden we saw them dive down and they started to fire at us. A lady ran out of her house and pulled us indoors and we all got under her table.'

Dr Annie Thomson risked her life to administer first aid to a man trapped deep in the wreckage of a Glasgow house after a raid in March 1941. 'I was working in my clinic when I received an urgent message for assistance,' Thomson told a newspaper a few days later. 'I was told groans had been heard coming from among the wreckage. Pausing only to be sure that my morphia syringe was loaded I hurried to the spot.'

Rescue workers warned Dr Thomson that the wreckage was unstable and the victim was probably dead by now. Thomson nonetheless crawled into the ruins of the house and located the man. 'His left leg was pinned under wreckage,' she said. 'I gave him an injection of morphia in the left arm, the only arm I could reach.' It took rescue workers three hours to free the man. He died on the way to hospital but another man found nearby survived. 'The blinding, choking dust was the worst of it, but I was only too anxious to help the poor man,' Dr Thomson said. 'I never thought about the possibility of the wreckage caving in.'

Some people were even prepared to risk their lives to rescue pets terrorised by the bombing. The Chelsea branch of the Our Dumb Friends' League provided a home during the height of the Blitz to 88 dogs, 824 cats and 21 birds. Most were found by some of their female superintendents, one of whom described what happened during one particularly heavy raid: 'I cycled along Royal Hospital Road, advising the wardens and some rescued (people) to send their animals to the shelter. On my way to the church at 5.00am, I rescued a scared and scratchy kitten from a shop and met a weeping man who took me to his ruined shop, where his dog needed attention. After staying with him for an hour, I continued my journey. I made five journeys with my bicycle. Then a taximan saw me "punctured" and loaded with two baskets and a kitten, and generously conveyed us to Bywater Street.'

* * *

'This is an age of false values and quack doctrines. Millions of children are brought up in cotton wool; they are pampered and petted by over-indulgent parents; they grow up undisciplined and untrained for the parts they have to play as men and women in a hard world . . . they are afraid to look life in the face, so they try to bury their heads in amusement. In a word, this is an effeminate and spineless generation. Gone are the days when youth walked hand in hand with adventure. The pioneer has been replaced by the lounge lizard, and the lad fresh from school prefers to accept a miserable pittance from the State rather than strike out for himself.'

No, not a Norman Tebbit column in the *Daily Telegraph*, but comments published in the *Belfast Telegraph* on 24 June 1937 by a twenty-four-year-old using the *nom de plume* Max Winchester. He was afraid to reveal his true identity, presumably in case he was slapped by an enraged lounge lizard. The *Belfast Telegraph* disclosed only that its columnist had a public-school education and was employed in his father's office on the Stock Exchange.

While Winchester deplored the effeminacy of his sex, the constitution of young women was also being questioned. Two reports in early 1939, one by the Birmingham Commission and another by the Inter-Departmental Committee, expressed concern about the recruitment shortage in nursing. The report's authors sniffily listed the reasons why young recruits to nursing were dropping out: 'over-harsh discipline amounting almost to tyranny, petty restrictions upon reasonable liberty, and complete disregard of personal convenience in the arrangement of such matters as study hours, time off and holidays'. In other words, the young women of 1939 lacked the selflessness and determination of their mothers' generation.

It all sounds very familiar – the country going to the dogs because the youth of today are lazy good-for-nothings . . . etc., etc. Yet when Britain declared war on Germany on 3 September, the Civil Defence numbered 1.5 million volunteers, tens of thousands of whom were young women who were now called up to serve as part-time firewomen, ambulance drivers, firewatchers and nurses.

The lounge lizards and young lads sponging off the state joined the military and proved they were anything but an 'effeminate and spineless generation'.

Hillary's memoir, *The Last Enemy*, became an instant classic of its genre. JB Priestley wrote that the value of the book 'lies in the fact that it is the statement of a fully articulate young man about life in a service which is generally inarticulate'.

Unlike many war memoirs, *The Last Enemy* has aged well because its essence is less about combat and more about human nature – that of a self-absorbed, cynical young man who was scornful of anyone outside his echo chamber of conceited values.

* * *

War opened Hillary's mind and he understood the shallowness of the selfish. For a fleeting moment, as Britain locked down in March, it appeared that the country might come together in a spirit of selflessness. When the NHS appealed for 250,000 volunteers to help the nation's most vulnerable, three times that number stepped up and, for a few glorious weeks, we forgot about the inane vanity of pop stars, footballers and minor celebrities and instead lavished our devotion on doctors and nurses and other key workers. Others acted on their own initiative, like Caroline Smith, in Ulverston, Cumbria, who launched a 'Self-Isolation Group' in which volunteers provided meals and went shopping for people self-isolating.

It was joyous and it was refreshing. But, alas, this spirit of selflessness struggled to breach the walls of British bureaucracy. Nowhere was this more evident than in the failure to reopen the vast majority of schools, leaving children without a proper education for several months, despite the fact that the under-15s had a 1 in 3.5 million chance of dying of COVID-19. The Government was weak in the face of the intransigence of unions, who, in the opinion of the former Labour Education Secretary David Blunkett, were 'working against the interests of children'. Teaching unions said their members were concerned about the health risks, an issue that didn't frighten teachers during the Second World War.

Then they were selfless in their endeavours to ensure children continued to receive an education. One teacher, Berwick Sayers, recalled how in the countryside there weren't enough schools for all the evacuated children, so 'for weeks in some cases, teachers and children assembled at some agreed point and walked the country lanes until they could be housed in some suitable hall'.

Teachers were just as diligent in the cities. At a meeting of the Brentford and Chiswick Education Committee in November 1940, the chairman, Alderman Maurice Leahy, made a point of thanking the teachers for their 'gallant' behaviour since the start of the Blitz two months earlier. 'Those who had had to go away had gone willingly and voluntarily, while others who had stayed behind were doing very fine work with the little that was left them of the old system,' said the chairman. 'The teachers, every one of them, had all done very valuable work.'

When Belfast was subjected to a series of heavy air raids in the spring of 1941, the schools were temporarily closed, so the teachers en masse 'responded to an appeal to help in the work of catering for homeless and relieving tired workers'.

In Rochdale in the summer of 1940, so many teachers signed up to moonlight for the civil defence that the County Committee was obliged to remind them that, while they were proud of their public spirit, they must not forget that the classroom was their priority.

The lockdown took away people's liberty but it gave them a fresh perspective on kindness. It's easy to tweet a '#Bekind' hashtag on social media, but actually performing acts of kindness – particularly during a pandemic – is more of a challenge. It was one to which millions of Brits rose during the lockdown as they came together to look out for each other – in the same way that Gladys Shaw did in the Blitz.

It was a much-needed reminder about the superficiality of social media; that the 'friends' and 'followers' one accumulates on those platforms are, for the most part, meaningless. Social media is increasingly 'anti-social', a place where fake news and vile views flourish. The Internet hasn't brought people together, as was the hope; it has set them against each other, fomenting an online tribal warfare; and, above all, it's created a cult of the individual at the expense of a community. As its creator, Tim Berners-Lee, said in a 2018 interview, the Internet 'has evolved into an engine of inequity and division'.

What struck me most about Gladys Shaw was her contentment. She had found fulfilment in devoting her life to others, the most downtrodden people on Earth. She hadn't done it for money, acclaim or vanity, but from her innate selflessness, and her reward was a serenity that

Richard Hillary came to know in the last months of his life. 'To whom would I address this book?' he wrote on the last page of *The Last Enemy*. 'To Humanity . . . for Humanity must be the public of any book. Yes, that despised Humanity which I had so scorned and ridiculed.'

6

Courage

I'll never forget the day in 2004 when I met Gillian Tanner. She preferred to be called 'Bobbie', she told me, shortly after she met me off the bus in Aberaeron on the Welsh coast. We drove to her home at Ciliau Aeron, what I described in my diary as: 'A big, ramshackle house in the hills. It's an absolute mess, populated by seven ugly poodles. Unkempt, untidy and reeking of dogs, but charming in an inexplicable way.'

Quite soon into our conversation, Bobbie told me she had been twice married and twice divorced, with both men as feckless as each other. And she also expressed her conviction that her mother was a lesbian. That's a conversation stopper, if ever there was one.

I described Bobbie in my diary as a 'dying breed, and one of the most extraordinary people I've ever met'.

She was also one of the bravest. Truly, she was a fearless woman, who competed in the Monte Carlo Rally on four occasions in the 1950s. But it was her exploits behind the wheel of a fire brigade vehicle that had led me to her door.

Bobbie had had an itinerant upbringing. Her father – also feckless – abandoned his family when she was a baby and she was raised by her well-connected mother, whose passions were horse racing and gambling and, apparently, other women. Bobbie was sent to France aged twelve to learn the language, and at seventeen she was despatched to Germany, where her uncle was a naval attaché. She attended the Berlin Olympics in 1936 and was jostled by some young Nazis who found her lipstick immoral. On the day that war was declared, Bobbie drove to London in her BSA car and volunteered for the fire service. With her pedigree, she expected to be posted to Chelsea but Bobbie was ordered to Station N61 in the docklands.

When the station commander learned that Bobbie was an accomplished driver, he threw her the keys of the 30-cwt petrol lorry. Her job during the air raids was to drive to blazing buildings and fill up trailer pumps as the firemen tackled the infernos. The petrol was stored in two-gallon tins stacked on wooden shelves inside the lorry. One spark from a German incendiary bomb – which fizzed out magnesium at 2,500 degrees Celsius – and Bobbie would have been barbecued.

She tucked away such thoughts at the back of her mind. When the Blitz started on 7 September 1940, she was in the thick of the action, driving her petrol lorry to the docks that were being targeted by hundreds of Luftwaffe bombers. Roads were often blocked with debris or by craters, so Bobbie had to find another route to the fire, the petrol tins on the shelves behind her rattling as she negotiated the bombed-out streets.

The raid of 20 September 1940 was particularly bad. According to one newspaper report that described Bobbie's feat this evening: 'Six serious fires were raging and bombing was intense. For three hours, she went from fire to fire driving a 30-cwt lorry loaded with 150 gallons of petrol with which to replenish supplies.'

In recognition of her bravery, Bobbie became the first firewoman to receive the George Medal. She collected her decoration from King George VI in February 1941 at Buckingham Palace. Outside the Palace, she was asked about her bravery by a reporter from the *Daily Herald*. 'It was nothing much.' she replied. 'I merely obeyed orders.'

Other newspapers wanted to know more about her – what did she do when off-duty? Baking, perhaps, or did she like to knit? No, said Bobbie, hunting and riding were her hobbies. The papers stuck to the sexist stereotypes, much to the irritation of the Women's Auxiliary Fire Service newsletter. In its edition of February 1941, it congratulated Bobbie on her medal and remarked: 'Though to read some newspaper accounts, one would think it was almost equally due to her capacity for knitting without dropping stitches during a raid.'

Bobbie drove her petrol lorry for the duration of the Blitz until the final raid on 10 May 1941. That was a hellish attack, which killed nearly 1,500 Londoners. Bobbie spent much of the night at the Peek Freans factory in Bermondsey, lugging the two-gallon tins of petrol (which when full weighed 17lb) from her lorry to the trailer pumps, and then pouring in the contents through a funnel. 'This was the trickiest moment, pouring in the petrol,' she told me. 'Because all it needed was a couple of drops on the engine and I would've gone up in flames.'

I asked her how she controlled her fear. She laughed. 'If it's going to happen, then it's going to happen and there's nothing you can do about it.'

Bobbie and I corresponded for a long while and in one letter she told me of her presence at a ceremony in Whitehall in July 2005 at which the Queen unveiled a 22ft-high bronze sculpture in Whitehall to commemorate the role of women during the Second World War. The driving force behind the long overdue memorial was Baroness Betty Boothroyd, the former Speaker of the House of Commons, and she presented Bobbie to the Queen. 'I must say that I found it a very moving ceremony,' said Bobbie.

At the inauguration ceremony, Baroness Boothroyd declared that the sculpture 'is dedicated to all the women who served our country and the cause of freedom in uniform and on the home front . . . It depicts the uniforms of women in the forces alongside the working clothes of those who worked in the factories, the hospitals, the emergency services and the farms'.

Each branch, each member, made a contribution to the war effort and, in nearly each case, the women surprised themselves with their courage. They had been brought up to believe they were the 'weaker sex' – physically and emotionally incapable of withstanding physical rigour, let alone displaying courage under fire.

On the day war was declared, Hermione Ranfurly confided her fear to her diary after driving home to Edinburgh from the Highlands. 'The windscreen wipers ticked to and fro and it seemed as if each swipe brought a new and more horrifying thought to me,' she wrote. 'We had started on a journey – but to where? And for how long?'

On the day the war in Europe ended, Hermione described the VE Day celebrations in London: 'Through a giant carnival of dancing, singing and laughing people I made my way home with a thousand thoughts rushing through my head – of the marvellous people I'd met, of the wounded, the dead, the animals, of the jokes, and the tears; the hopes and the fears; of those terrible, frightening, yet triumphant years.'

For most of the war, Hermione had been stationed in the Middle East, working first as a secretary for the Special Operations Executive (SOE), an espionage and sabotage agency, and later as the PA to General Henry Maitland Wilson, the Supreme Allied Commander in the Mediterranean. Her husband had spent three years as a prisoner of war and yet, despite the anxiety, danger and pressure, she had prospered as a woman and discovered she was capable of so much.

Hermione Ranfurly and Bobbie Tanner came from the same class, society girls who had already developed a modicum of self-confidence. But the courage of women cut across all classes among the Greatest Generation, and it manifested itself in a variety of forms.

The courage of Daphne Pearson and Joan Aldridge was instinctive. Aldridge was a member of the Land Army in Oxfordshire when she saw a wounded RAF pilot parachute into the River Thames. Leaping into the water, she saved the pilot's life.

The twenty-nine-year-old Pearson, from St Ives in Cornwall, had been a photographer before joining the WAAF as a medical orderly on the outbreak of war. On 31 May 1940, an RAF bomber exploded as it landed in Kent and the chain of subsequent events was described in the *Cornishman* newspaper in August 1940: 'Rushing towards the plane, Corporal Pearson [as she then was] disregarded the fact that it was ablaze, and the imminent risk of exploding bombs. Shaking the partially stunned pilot into consciousness, she dragged him some distance from the machine. Whilst she was divesting him of his parachute harness, the bomb exploded and, in order to protect the pilot from the blast and splinters, Miss Pearson threw herself upon him.'

For her heroism, Daphne received the Empire Gallantry Medal, which the following year was replaced by the George Cross. Daphne was the first woman to receive the new decoration.

The courage of Phyllis 'Pippa' Latour was of a different kind. Not instinctive, but ice cold, requiring supreme self-control of the sort Bobbie Tanner displayed every night during the Blitz. Pippa was eighteen when war broke out, although so small in stature she could pass as a twelve-year-old. She joined the WAAF as a flight mechanic but the SOE swiftly saw her potential. Her late father was French and she spoke the language like a native. She accepted the invitation to train with the SOE in the belief that they wanted to employ her as a translator; after the first round of training, Pippa was asked by the SOE if she fancied parachuting into France as a spy. 'They said I could have three days to think about it,' she recalled. 'I told them I didn't need three days to make a decision ... I'd take the job now.'

On 1 May 1944, Pippa parachuted into Calvados, where she was met by the Maquis. They provided her with a bicycle and, for the next few weeks, she pedalled around the countryside posing as a fourteen-year-old French girl who had relocated to Normandy to escape the bombing of Paris. On one occasion, she was picked up in a sweep of a village and subjected to a strip search by the Germans. Pippa even had to remove her silk hair ribbon so her hair could be searched. Had the Germans examined the ribbon itself they would have seen a set of radio codes printed in minute lettering.

The information that Pippa radioed back to England was crucial in the planning of D-Day, and yet despite her heroics she never told her four children about her wartime activities. They didn't learn of their mother's courage until 2000 when one of her sons saw something about her on the Internet.

* * *

The common thread in the courage displayed by Latour, Pearson and Tanner was that they risked their own lives. They were prepared to put their bodies on the line, as were many other men and women during the Second World War. The civilians on the home front – those in the towns and cities subjected to German bombing – were faced with a game of risk during every raid. Where to seek shelter? In the under-ground, in a street shelter, in the Anderson shelter in the backyard or better to 'take a chance' by staying put at home?

A surprising number chose the latter, like the Levy family in Battersea. 'We had a brick air-raid shelter in our tiny backyard but it was so cold and damp we preferred to stay indoors and take our chances,' Joyce Levy told me. She was seven at the time, and 'quite happy sleeping under the kitchen table with my teddy bear and cat for company. Whenever a bomb came down a bit too close for comfort, I had three heads joining me – Mum, Gran and Grandad. They used to say that if ever we get hit, our behinds would be blown off, which used to make me giggle.'

The Levys and countless other families weighed up the options and decided to risk staying at home. It was their choice, not the Government's, which didn't force people into official shelters during an air raid. They warned them of the potential dangers (they significantly over-estimated the death rates as it turned out) in pamphlets distributed to every household in 1939. But the people were free to assess the risk and make their own decision about where to seek shelter in the event of a raid.

Initially, the authorities tried to prevent Londoners sheltering on the platforms of Underground stations during raids because they feared a 'deep shelter mentality' would take hold, which, in the words of Sir John Anderson, the

Home Secretary in June 1940, might 'affect the morale and spirit of the people'. But the Government relented when the Blitz began three months later; it was the people's choice to decide where they wished to shelter.

A similar philosophy characterised the planning behind Operation Dynamo, the evacuation of 330,000 British and French soldiers from Dunkirk. Nearly 700 civilian boats participated in the rescue in response to an appeal from the Admiralty. None of them sailed having first carried out a risk assessment; they headed across the Channel to France, aware of the danger, but in the hope that they would return with their human cargo intact.

'It is boring to bang on about the war, but hard not to do so, because it was the last period at which our leaders faced similar huge life-and-death decisions,' wrote the historian Max Hastings in *The Times* during the COVID-19 crisis. 'Every course involved risk. Duty required ministers and commanders to choose the least bad from a range of unwelcome options, accepting the need to pay a price in lost lives in the greater interest of the nation.'

It wasn't only ministers and commanders during the war who were compelled to wrestle with risk. On 1 September 1939, Operation Pied Piper began – the mass evacuation of British children from their city homes to the countryside. Evacuation was voluntary – the Government left it to mums and dads to decide whether to put their offspring on a train or keep them at home in London, Glasgow, Manchester, and so on. The Government, who for months had warned the people of likely heavy aerial attacks within hours of war being declared, had expected three million evacuees in the first week (including expectant mothers, the sick and the blind) but they registered only 1,317,000.

When the air raids failed to materialise – a period that was dubbed the 'Sitzkrieg' in some quarters – the evacuees began to drift home. Walter Elliot, the Minister of Health, told people to stay put: 'Don't think it all right because nothing has happened yet,' he said in the middle of September.

When that had no effect, the Queen was enlisted, appealing over the airwaves 'to her fellow parents to keep the children in the country'. Few listened. Parents weighed up the risks, and decided they would bring their children home. In some cases, their decision was made easier by accounts of the uncivil reception their children had received in the countryside.

By Christmas 1939, the Ministry of Health reported that 45 per cent of evacuees had returned. In London at the start of 1940, there were 200,000 schoolchildren at a loose end. Schools had been closed the previous September but many teachers (including some who came out of retirement) volunteered to return to the classroom to solve the problem.

The *Sunday Mirror*, for one, was outraged and demanded in its edition of 14 January 1940 that these children be forcibly evacuated. 'It is not right that the lives of people in a war like this should be left entirely in their own hands,' said the paper. 'Is [the Government] going to allow millions of women and children to imperil their existence entirely at their own free will? Evacuation could be made compulsory.'

The Government refused to bow to media hysteria, adamant that the final choice rested with the parents; it was their right to weigh up the risk.

Britons in 2020 were given no choice about going into lockdown. There was no liberty to decide whether one wanted to 'take their chance' with the virus; the nation was ordered to take shelter even though data indicated it was not a serious disease for the young and the healthy. For a tantalising couple of weeks, the Government had been willing to risk 'herd immunity', on the advice of its scientific advisers, but then it lost its collective nerve, caving in to media pressure and other scientific voices.

The problem is that today's political and media class grew up as the culture of 'safetyism' took root in Britain, and they have passed their aversion to risk on to their children, which is why many of today's young are derided as 'snowflakes'. But is it their fault they take shelter in safe spaces if they've been reared from the cradle to be fearful of everyone and everything?

One of the most famous wartime SAS officers was Roy Farran, DSO, MC & Two Bars, as ruthless as he was courageous. In dismissing one young officer who failed to meet the required standard, Farran described him as 'weak, wet and windy', an apt assessment of what millions of Britons now are. We've been infantilised to such a degree that train station announcers remind us to drink water when it's hot and warn us that rain causes platforms to become wet. Broadcasters are no better with their warnings before programmes about 'flash photography' and 'outdated attitudes', treating us all as if we're five years old.

In 2006, Hugh Cunningham, Emeritus Professor of Social History at the University of Kent, published *The Invention of Childhood* in which he described the crucial difference between childhood in twenty-first-century Britain and childhood in previous generations: 'Children in the past have been assumed to have capabilities that we now rarely think they have . . . So fixated are we on giving our children a long and happy childhood that we downplay their abilities and their resilience.'

The resilience, for example, displayed by Joyce Levy under her kitchen table during the Blitz, or of Dennis Robbins, who was a nine-year-old schoolboy in London at the same time. 'The memory that sticks out in my mind was the manner in which we schoolchildren accepted the loss of our friends following the raids,' he told me in a letter. 'We would go to our infant school in Old Woolwich Road and barely be concerned that there were empty desks where some of our friends sat but who had perished the night before. One would hear the comment that Charlie's or Bert's house had been hit by a land mine or similar. No tears, no counselling . . . we got on with our lives.'

Despite the scare stories emanating daily during the COVID-19 crisis from the political and media class, millions of Brits refused to be cowed. Increasingly, as the lockdown wore on, people – particularly the young – weighed up the risks and came to the conclusion that they were willing to 'take a chance' on the outside. Some went on Black Lives Matter marches, others crowded onto beaches or attended raves and many simply met up with friends. They were criticised in some quarters – often, ironically, by middle-aged media commentators who, prior to the pandemic, had mocked the 'snowflake' generation.

The British character hasn't changed that much over the decades. There have always been risk-takers and risk-avoiders, just as there have always been those who cope well and a minority who crack. In her book, *England's Hour*, published in 1941, Vera Brittain relayed a conversation she had had with a London ambulance driver after a heavy air raid. 'It's queer,' she says, 'how differently people I've known all my life have taken it. Half an hour after it was over, some of them were out shopping as though nothing had happened. Others have been so apprehensive ever since that, the moment the siren goes, they rush for the shelter.'

'Project Fear' was a phrase coined in 2014 in the lead-up

to the Scottish independence referendum, and then again when Britain voted on EU membership. It returned for a third time in 2020 with the Government's 'Stay Home, Protect the NHS, Save Lives' message, which was relentlessly pushed in press conferences and in the media.

In fact, Project Fear is nothing new; it was deployed by the British Government at the start of the Second World War as a means of controlling the people. The dire warnings about the likely devastating consequences of enemy air raids were intended to make the population more malleable when it came to rationing, evacuation and sheltering.

It was only partly successful because all Project Fears have a limited shelf life. Why? Contrary to what politicians and civil servants believe, we Brits aren't stupid – we're discerning. In 1939, the people heeded the warnings but, when the air raids started, they realised they weren't as destructive as the Government had forecast; it was the same in 2020 with COVID-19. The virus wasn't as deadly as some people had made out. Indeed, according to analysis conducted by Sir David Spiegelhalter, Chair of the Winton Centre for Risk and Evidence Communication at the University of Cambridge, the under-fifties are more likely to die from an accident or injury than COVID-19.

Life, ultimately, is about risk; as Bobbie Tanner once said, 'If it's going to happen, then it's going to happen . . . and there's nothing you can do about it.'

7

Vitality

In September 2017, I visited Jim Booth at his home in Taunton. When we had spoken the previous week, we agreed a time of 10.30am but, on my arrival, there was no one at home. 'Oh no,' I thought. 'The old boy's forgotten.' I rang the bell again. After all, at ninety-six, it must take him a few minutes to shuffle to the door. But still no response.

Then a car pulled into the driveway, and out jumped Jim. He was dressed in shorts and a t-shirt, and was wearing a pair of muddy boots. 'Gavin? Nice to meet you. Sorry I'm a little late, I was digging up carrots on my allotment.' There were two boxes of carrots in the boot. Jim had clearly had a productive morning. 'If you could carry one inside, I'd be grateful. Then I'll put on the kettle and we'll talk. What is it you want to know?'

I wanted to know about Jim's war, and specifically his involvement in D-Day when, as a member of a Royal Navy special forces unit, he had a front-row seat for the invasion.

Jim's house was a treasure trove of wartime memorabilia and he was off to Normandy in a couple of weeks on a commemorative trip. He was a regular at such events, at home and abroad, and in 2015 his photo had adorned the national press when he danced with Camilla, Duchess of Cornwall, at a Royal British Legion reception in the College Gardens of Westminster Abbey.

Jim told me that he'd inherited his irreverence from his Anglo-Irish mother, Mary, who had married Charles in July 1919. Jim was born two years later, two days after the death of his sister, Julia, aged eleven months.

Perhaps that tragedy accounts to a degree for Jim's vitality – he's living for two. He was schooled at Eton, where his twin loves were music and rowing and, in September 1939, he went up to Cambridge but lasted less than a term before enlisting in the Navy as an ordinary seaman. 'I had a lovely time in the Navy looking back,' he told me. 'We'd go ashore and meet girls, and all the girls love a sailor! At Eton, I didn't know anything about girls. It was a wonderful window on to another aspect of England.'

Jim breezed through training. 'I'd been to boarding school,' he reminded me. 'That toughens you up.' At his training camp in Skegness, in what had been a Butlin's camp before the war, Jim's fellow seamen were working-class lads. They got on like a house on fire. Jim had no airs or graces, and his enthusiasm was infectious.

Jim was eventually commissioned as a sub-lieutenant to *HMS Turquoise*, an anti-submarine warfare trawler patrolling the North Sea. It was, he recalled, 'hot as hell' with regular attacks from German aircraft and motor torpedo boats. After a while, Jim was transferred to another ship, which was sent to Africa, and there he became restless. 'It was boring, doing the same old bloody routine day after day,' he said. 'So I wrote a silly letter to the Admiralty asking for something more exciting, please.'

The Admiralty obliged, and Jim was posted to a special forces unit called Combined Operation Assault Pilotage Parties, abbreviated to COPP by its select members. 'Here I was among a different breed,' said Jim. 'They were mad, but in a nice way.'

Jim fitted right in.

COPP was the brainchild of Lt Commander Nigel Clogstoun-Willmott, who had been inspired by the stories told to him as a child by his uncle, who had survived the shambles of the Gallipoli landings in 1915. Ignorance of the Turkish defences – natural and military – had contributed to the disastrous Allied invasion; Clogstoun-Willmott's idea was a small, highly-trained naval reconnaissance force that would gather intelligence on potential landing beaches prior to an assault.

It was a unit that harnessed technological advances both in naval warfare and in the intellect of its sailors. Jim was not uncommon among his generation – intelligent, irreverent and intrepid. He could think for himself, which was what COPP wanted.

On Jim's mantelpiece was a model of his midget submarine, *X-23*. He described its specifications, how it dived and how it surfaced, where they slept, what they ate, the smell, the noise and the claustrophobia of being one of five men inside a 52ft-long submarine. He even explained the procedure for going to the loo, which for a six-footer like Jim was no easy feat.

Then we talked about D-Day. The task of *X-23* and its crew was to guide the Anglo-Canadian fleet on to Sword Beach, the most easterly of the five invasion beaches. They had sailed from Portsmouth on the evening of Friday, 2 June and arrived at their target on the morning of 4 June. Through the periscope they could see the spire of Ouistreham church half a mile away. Happy with their position, the submarine dropped a small anchor and bottomed. They surfaced that evening and received a signal from England that the invasion had been postponed for twenty-four hours.

They bottomed again. Oxygen was now a concern. The air in *X-23* was fetid. Tension was high. They surfaced at nightfall on 5 June and received a message that the invasion was on. They bottomed once more, rose at 4.45am on 6 June and assembled the lights to seaward. Jim had planned to erect a second set of lights using a dinghy but the sea was too rough. Instead, he stood on the deck in the dark, waiting and listening. 'We had no idea of the size of the operation because, all the way through the build-up, the secrecy was incredible and so no one knew what the next person was doing,' said Jim. 'So we knew it was the real thing but we had no inkling of its size.'

At 5.07am, *X-23* began flashing her lights. Fifty minutes later, dawn broke on the Normandy coast. 'Suddenly, we saw them and it was a case of "Bloody hell, look at that lot," said Jim. 'It was literally ships as far as the eye could see. Spectacular. Then after a while, we went down inside because it was a bit cold and miserable out on deck. We put the kettle on and just waited.'

Jim subsequently served in the Far East with COPP, and had what he described as a couple of 'hairy moments' with the Japanese as he reconnoitred beaches on the west coast of Burma. Did you enjoy the war, I asked? 'Bloody loved it,' he replied without hesitation.

Before we went to the pub for lunch, Jim showed me his garden. Beyond it was a school playing field. 'I jog round there most days,' he told me. 'And usually cycle to the shops.'

I recall all this because I described it in my diary, as I did our conversation at lunch. We discussed, among other things, Brexit and transgender toilets. It was, I wrote, 'the most extraordinary encounter' with a man who 'talks and walks like one half his age'. I added: 'Oh, I do love that generation.'

* * *

Such vitality isn't unique to Jim among his generation. As we saw during the COVID-19 crisis, Captain Tom Moore is made of similar stuff, as is the Queen. Mike Sadler, also a centenarian, and the last remaining SAS veteran from the summer of 1942, visited France in 2019 to pay his respects to fallen comrades, and ninety-nine-year-old Lofty Carr – who knew Mike from their time together in the LRDG in 1941 – isn't as mobile as he once was, but his zest for life remains undimmed. Saddened to be separated from their friends during the lockdown, Lofty and his wife, Barbara, spent a lot of time in their front garden so they could hail passers-by.

Among veterans now no longer with us, I saw similar vitality in the twilight of their lives. Men and women always beetling about, keeping themselves busy, curious, energetic and optimistic. I remember well the day in 2004 when I visited Patrick Kinna's flat in Brighton to hear his account of working as Winston Churchill's stenographer during the Second World War. Unfortunately, we had got our wires crossed and Patrick, then a very dapper ninety years old, was expecting me the following week. It wasn't possible on this particular day because he was entertaining a friend. I passed the young gentleman on the stairs on my way out, and I understood what entertainment Patrick had in mind.

The irony is that when these old men were young, the greybeards of the day sneered at their sloth and labelled them 'lounge lizards'. In an annual footballers' service in St Paul's Church, Kingston, in November 1937, the Rev A Wellesley Orr thundered from the pulpit that Britain is 'turning out a race of blue stockings and wet socks . . . a soft generation that has too many lounge lizards, film fans and effeminate young men'.

It was true that the Greatest Generation were the first to take fashion seriously across all classes – the wireless and the cinema were partly responsible, and so, too, the tabloid newspapers that carried adverts for cosmetics and clothes. But appearances were deceptive. Beneath the frippery were tough young men and women, particularly the working class, who possessed far more steel than the middle-class vicars, politicians and journalists deriding them as lounge lizards.

Arthur 'Tommo' Thomson, who spent his war as a commando and SAS trooper, was born into poverty in west London in 1920. 'There were times I didn't go to school because I had no shoes. Sometimes I went in my dad's slippers,' he told me. 'I left school aged thirteen and a half and went to work in Covent Garden delivering fruit to the country markets: Devizes, Hereford, Abergavenny. We left Covent Garden at five in the morning, got to the market at nine, set up the stall and sold the produce and then returned home. We often drove more than 1,000 miles in a week.'

When I got to know Tommo in 2002, he was working part-time as a greenkeeper at his local golf course. 'I enjoy the work at the golf course,' he said. 'I don't want to sit indoors in my rocking chair . . . that's not for me.'

Tommo had been sent out to earn a crust from early adolescence; it was what was expected of working-class lads. The girls were expected to marry and settle down. But the Greatest Generation weren't like their mums. The world was changing and there were opportunities for young women to strike out on their own and become independent.

The feminist author Vera Brittain was given a tour by an official from the Ministry of Labour of a workshop in south London in 1940 that was now a training centre for women engineers. The young women on the benches came from all walks of life: an actress, a shop assistant at Harrods, a nursery school teacher and a student at the London School of Economics. One, who described herself as 'just a married woman', told Brittain what she enjoyed about constructing a spanner: 'I find I can do things with my hands I never even thought of. That's what I like.'

I have a file bulging with letters I received in 2004. I was researching a book about the London Blitz and I placed a few adverts in relevant magazines requesting survivors' stories. The response was incredible. Some 200 letters flooded in from around the world: Canada, South Africa, the United States, New Zealand and Australia, as well as every corner of the UK. Most were from women, nearly all were handwritten and every one glowed with vitality.

One correspondent, Una Quibell, originally from west London but, in 2004, a resident of Pefferlaw in Ontario, began by asking me to forgive her handwriting but she was 'nearly eighty-three and my hands have arthritis'. Una had then written five pages of eloquent testimony about her Blitz experiences. She'd worked in a munitions factory in Hayes, Middlesex, and ended her letter with a request: 'Please put us munitions girls in [the book]. I've never seen us in any book and I think we were on the front line. We had to stand at our benches when [the Germans] came over.'

The pride Una rightly felt was replicated in countless other letters from women who had worked tirelessly as telephone operators, ambulance drivers, firewatchers, nurses, air-raid wardens, served in the ATS, WVS, WRNS, WAAF or Land Army.

One of the few letters I received from a man was from Ron Pory, a serviceman who one evening in 1940 was waiting for a bus at the depot in West Norwood when an air raid began.

'The Germans started dropping clusters of incendiary bombs and these would burst into many fragment pieces and set fire to anything near,' wrote Ron. 'And, of course, they burst sending fluorescent pieces under the buses. The cleaning ladies could at any time have gone to an air-raid shelter, but not these Cockney Londoners. They were out there with their brooms and long rods dragging the pieces of phosphorus bombs out from under the buses into the centre of the road and then tipping buckets of sand over the phosphorus pieces. It's these ladies that England should be proud of.'

The pre-war scepticism of the older generation gave way to an admiration for the young men and women doing their bit for Britain. 'We were all an improvement on our unendangered selves,' wrote JB Priestley. 'No longer suspicious of gaiety, we almost sparkled. What more than half the English fear and detest is not threatened disaster, material insecurity, sacrifice or danger, but boredom. They should be offered crises, not guarantees of prosperity and security.'

Enrolment in evening classes rose dramatically during the war. In Edinburgh, reported the *Scotsman* in October 1940, there was a 42 per cent increase in attendance compared to the previous year, with music and physical education the most popular. 'The students are mostly young people,' reported the newspaper. 'Older people are still chary of going out in the blackout.'

The novelist William Sansom was a fireman in London during the Blitz and, in 1947, reflected on his wartime experience. 'In war, certain responsibilities are shrugged off or postponed,' he wrote. 'Others are assumed, but of a different, a more vivid, a shorter-lived nature. There are sensations of a new virility, of paradoxical freedom, and of a rather bawdy "live-for-today" philosophy.'

This philosophy was an understandable by-product of the war for a young generation that experienced death, mutilation and misery on an unprecedented scale; the Second World War was the first conflict in which, for the British people, the home front was also a battleground, with thousands dying and suffering life-changing injuries.

The vitality of the Greatest Generation, their 'live-for-today' philosophy, remained with them for life. Arthur Thomson, who died in his eighty-ninth year, attributed his longevity to 'wine, women, song . . . and twenty fags a day'. Nevertheless, he admitted, he would often cry into his whisky of an evening when he thought of his pal, Doug Eccles, a member of the SAS, who was tortured and executed by the Nazis in 1944.

But there was also a virtuousness to the vitality; it wasn't just about living for the moment. Two wartime operations are proof of this. The first, Operation Pied Piper, was launched on 1 September 1939, the objective being to evacuate children from Britain's major cities. The operation kicked off at the crack of dawn and children were soon leaving London train stations at the rate of 8,000 an hour. In Glasgow, an estimated 75,000 children had departed for the Highlands by late afternoon. In total, half a million were evacuated in one day (three million in four days), in what *The Times* described on 2 September as 'a triumph of preparation, organization, and discipline'.

In contrast, the Government was too incompetent to organise the return of school pupils for the final four weeks of the 2020 summer term after Britain emerged from the lockdown. They weren't helped by the politicking of some teachers' unions, who exhibited a marked reluctance to co-operate in ensuring children – who it was reported in June were more likely to be hit by lightning than die of COVID-19 – didn't spend six months out of the classroom.

The organisation and discipline that characterised Operation Pied Piper was again evident in May 1940 when 330,000 British and French soldiers were evacuated from Dunkirk as part of Operation Dynamo. Admiral Bertram Ramsay had a week to plan Dynamo, which required assembling an evacuation fleet of nearly 1,000 vessels. 'We were told to get out as many as we could in forty-eight hours,' he explained after the operation. 'All our plans were made on that basis. We set aside room here with about seven telephones and fifteen or sixteen fellows working in it.'

Contrast Pied Piper and Dynamo with the shambles of Britain's response to the COVID-19 crisis. In February 2020, routine testing and tracing of contacts was abandoned because Public Health England's systems could only cope with five COVID-19 cases a week; and according to a report from the Scientific Advisory Group on Emergencies, this was with 'modelling suggesting it might only be possible to increase this to fifty cases'. The Government's NHS contact-tracing app was also a fiasco; originally scheduled for deployment in mid-May, teething problems delayed its launch and it was finally scrapped in June after being found ineffective.

So inefficient was the NHS's distribution of personal protective equipment [PPE] that the army was drafted in, and they were reportedly horrified at the 'appalling' organisation they found.

There was also a marked lack of vitality over the Government's response to travellers arriving in Britain. While countries such as Canada and New Zealand swiftly imposed stringent restrictions on travel, Britain did nothing, allowing people to jet into the country from all over the world while its people were locked up in their homes. Then some bright spark in the Government suggested it would be a good idea to introduce a fourteen-day quarantine law on 8 June, by which time the pandemic was way past its peak.

And what about the tyranny of the two-metre social distancing rule? While many countries listened to the advice of the World Health Organization and stipulated its citizens need keep no more one metre apart post-lockdown, Britain insisted on two, to the angst of business. Numerous scientists recommended that the two metres could be trimmed, so what did the Government do? It set up a commission to examine the pros and cons, as the clock ticked and the economy shrank further.

Similar incomprehensible inertia was displayed by the Royal National Lifeboat Institution (RNLI), roundly criticised after two people drowned on the May Bank Holiday weekend. Mark Dowie, the institution's Chief Executive, said he was 'very sad' at the deaths but refused to take responsibility for the failure to reinstate lifeguard patrols at 240 beaches after their suspension in March. 'Rolling out a lifeguard service – especially in a pandemic – is not as simple as putting a lifeguard on a beach,' he said in an open letter. 'We have to find PPE that will work on a beach and in the water – visors and aprons are no good on a rescue board. And we have to train our lifeguards in procedures to reduce the risk of infection. All this takes time.' In the meantime, said Dowie, the Government should 'restrict access to the coast'.

That sound you can hear is Admiral Ramsay turning in his grave.

It's a recurring theme in modern Britain that the listlessness, cowardice and dithering of our so-called 'élite' is in marked contrast with the strength, vitality and courage of the majority of the population. Admittedly, there is a minority who, taking their lead from officialdom, are apathetic and always ready to pass the buck.

But, in general, left to their own devices, and free from the infuriating and pointless bureaucracy that characterises much of British life, people are still eager to 'do their bit'. Look at the 750,000 men, women and children who signed up to be NHS volunteer responders, and the hundreds of mutual aid groups that were established to support neighbours in self-isolation under the umbrella organisation 'Covid-19 Mutual Aid UK'. 'People are self-organising with incredible efficiency, respect and creativity,' said one of the co-founders, Kelsey Mohamed.

Then there were the thousands who got off their backsides to raise money for one good cause or another. Tom Moore had already been lauded for his efforts, but at the other end of the age scale there was vitality every bit as impressive. Eleven-year-old Harry Swing said he was so inspired by 'Captain Tom' that he ran a full marathon over the course of four days to raise funds for his local hospice.

And in Scotland, thirteen-year-old Aiden Russell raised £700 to buy meals for NHS staff at Crosshouse Hospital by completing the Commando X-Fit Challenge, which entailed a 1-mile run, 100 burpees, 200 press-ups, 300 squats and another 1-mile run

In 1995, the American author Bill Bryson toured Britain and then wrote about the people in his best-selling book, *Notes from a Small Island*. Brits, he said approvingly, were noticeable for their 'tireless, dogged optimism'. They still are – or, at least, they are outside the Westminster Bubble.

Inside the 'Bubble', the glass is half empty; outside, it's half full.

Britain has just come through its biggest crisis since the war, albeit one of a very different nature. The coming years could well be economically tough, as they were after the Second World War, but we should take heart from how we adapted to the lockdown. The vitality, the initiative and the community spirit so frequently on display was a throwback to another era, an era many believed lay in the past. Not everyone, to paraphrase JB Priestley, 'sparkled' during the COVID-19 lockdown, but enough did to give us hope that there's life yet in the old British bulldog. Just as there's life still in Jim Booth.

Two months after I visited Jim Booth, he had another caller, a forty-year-old thug called Joseph Isaacs. He launched a vicious assault on Jim, battering his head and arms with a claw hammer before robbing him of a small amount of money. Jim was in court to see Isaacs sentenced to twenty years' imprisonment for what the judge called a brutal and senseless attack.

Jim's daughter read a family victim impact statement to the court. 'His faithful heart continues to beat at the core of our family,' she said. 'He remains unbowed, an unconquerable soul, and we look forward to many more happy and memorable times spent together.'

Outside the court, Jim spoke of his sadness at how a young man's life could have gone so wrong. He bore him no hatred. If anything, he was annoyed with himself. 'I blame myself because I was special services,' he told reporters. 'I think I should really have known how to deal with this but I didn't . . . I was too old, obviously.'

8

Integrity

I never met Porter Jarrell before his death in 2001, but I knew two men who served with him in the Special Boat Squadron (SBS). Dick Holmes still referred to him affectionately as 'the Yank' seventy years later. At Bari in southern Italy, recalled Holmes, Porter acquired two American footballs from some US troops and tried in vain to teach the SBS the finer points of the sport.

At around the time Porter instruction was falling flat, Simon Wingfield-Digby, the Conservative Member of Parliament for West Dorset, rose in the House of Commons to enquire of Winston Churchill whether it was the case 'that there is a body of men out in the Aegean Island, fighting under the Union flag, that are nothing short of being a band of murderous, renegade cut-throats'.

In reply to his Right Honourable Friend, the PM advised Wingfield-Digby, 'If you do not take your seat and keep quiet, I will send you out to join them.'

It would have been hard to find a more unlikely renegade 'cut-throat' than Porter Jarrell. Born in Canada in 1919 to American parents, Porter grew up in the States and graduated with a degree in Arts from the University of Middlebury in Vermont, subsequently finding employment with a music magazine in New York City.

Porter was a man of high moral principles. A conscientious objector, he nonetheless recognised the evil of Nazism and presented himself at a New York recruiting station after America declared war on Germany in December 1941. He was rejected on account of his flat feet and poor eyesight. Undeterred, Porter joined the American Field Service (AFS), an ambulance unit of volunteers (many conscientious objectors) that had served the Allied armies with great gallantry during the First World War.

Porter shipped out to North Africa in the summer of 1942 and his AFS unit was attached to the Eighth Army, serving with them from the battle of El Alamein to the end of the desert campaign in May 1943. In the last days of fighting, Porter saw one of his friends killed and several others wounded by shellfire. 'In a few short days, I think I saw much of the hell and terror that war can be,' he wrote home. 'They were all friends; and that is what war means.

But I think each one of us did a job, a job we asked to do, a job we wanted to do, a job badly needed, and none of us would refuse to volunteer again.'

In the summer of 1943, Porter volunteered for the SBS. They had just been formed from the SAS under the command of George Jellicoe, the son of the First World War admiral. Most of the men were Irish or gargantuan guardsmen, like Dick Holmes, who found the flat-footed and bespectacled American a source of curiosity.

Another medic was Norman Moran, an Anglo-Australian who most definitely was not a conscientious objector. He was trained in explosives, small arms and hand-to-hand combat.

Norman asked Porter how a man of his convictions had ended up in a special forces unit. 'He had been in the desert picking up wounded – of all nationalities – when they were caught by a German patrol,' Norman explained to me. 'They opened the back of the ambulance and a couple of Jerries opened fire and massacred the lot. Porter was so incensed by this that he came back to Cairo and joined a fighting unit.'

As outraged as he was, Porter refused to carry arms or participate in the SBS weapons training. Not that they were initially required on the island of Simi, north of Rhodes in the Aegean, where Porter was sent with twenty-six men of M Squadron in September 1943. For the first three weeks it was a sun-drenched idyll, but the Germans arrived at dawn on 7 October intent on wresting Simi from the British. Fighting raged throughout the day until the Germans withdrew, but the next day two Stuka dive-bombers attacked. One bomb demolished the SBS command post, trapping two men, Tom Bishop and Sydney Greaves, in the wreckage.

Sergeant Harold Whittle, a former miner, warned that the wrecked house was unstable and any attempt to rescue the men would risk a secondary collapse of debris. Porter believed it a risk worth taking. 'Jarrell, working with Sgt Whittle, worked for twenty-seven hours without rest to the point almost of collapse, exposing himself to extreme personal risk,' ran the citation for the George Medal awarded to the American. 'He continued work throughout two further raids when a bomb falling anywhere in the slightest vicinity would have brought the remnants of the building upon him. He was a source of inspiration to all the other workers.'

To free Bishop required the amputation of his leg. There was an RAF doctor present, but his wrist had been injured in the air raid so Porter volunteered to perform the task under instruction from the doctor. 'In appalling conditions, by candlelight, on his back, he did most of the leg amputation necessary,' explained Porter's citation. 'His movement was restricted by likelihood of the shored up debris falling on himself and the trapped man.'

Bishop and Greaves were freed eventually but, despite the courage of their rescuers, the pair died from their injuries.

Dick Holmes, who was awarded a Military Medal for his part in a raid on Crete in 1943, held Porter in the highest regard, as did every member of the SBS. A man of courage but, above all, integrity, Porter worked post-war for many years for the International Organization for Migration, a humanitarian concern he helped found and which he illuminated with his 'compassion and principle'.

Like Porter, the SBS commander, George Jellicoe, was admired and respected by all who served with him for his courage and integrity. In November 1943, Jellicoe and a squadron of SBS participated in the unsuccessful defence of another Aegean island, Leros, which eventually surrendered to the Germans on 16 November. Summoned to the command post of the island commander Brigadier Robert Tilney, Jellicoe was instructed to lay down his arms. He had no intention of complying with the feeble terms of what he called 'the Anglo-German Peace Conference'. Racing back to his men, Jellicoe oversaw their evacuation by boat to Turkey.

Jellicoe had been one of the first volunteers for the commandos when they were formed on the instruction of Winston Churchill in the summer of 1940. He was one of several rich and famous recruits; a few – notably Evelyn

Waugh and Randolph Churchill (the PM's son) – were roundly despised by the men they commanded. They coated their insecurity and inadequacy with an overweening obnoxiousness. But aristocrats such as Jellicoe and the Lords Sudeley and Stavordale were admired because they led by example.

Another young officer who set the highest standards of personal conduct was Sam Wilson. I interviewed Sam near the end of his long life, which had begun in September 1923 in Virginia. When Britain stood alone against the Nazis in 1940, Sam, then sixteen, sent Winston Churchill a poem pledging allegiance to Britain. By the time he received an effusive response from the Prime Minister, Wilson had lied about his age to enlist as a private in the Virginia National Guard.

In 1943, Sam answered a call for volunteers for a hazardous mission, and became one of 3,000 'Merrill's Marauders', named after their commander, the ineffectual Brigadier General Frank Merrill. Sam led one of the Marauders' reconnaissance platoons when they marched into Burma in February 1944 to fight a guerrilla war against the Japanese. He selected his men from the guardhouse. 'I had the sergeant call them out in one rank and I then walked down the line, shaking hands with each man and briefly talking to them,' he told me. 'I stepped back and told them what I was about, what I needed and that "it will be very dangerous, more dangerous than others, but we will have a front-row seat, and those who want to come with me, take three steps forward". And they did. I wanted men who regarded the business of losing their lives lightly, who were tougher than the tough.'

Sam was awarded two Silver Stars and a Bronze Star and remained in the army post-war, eventually retiring as a three-star general. Four Presidents – Nixon, Ford, Carter and George HW Bush – sought his counsel for its integrity and wisdom and, on retirement, Sam for many years was president of Hampden-Sydney College in Virginia at a time when its future was parlous.

He admired youth, and saw it as his duty to pass on his experiences to the students without judgement or bias. When Sam died in 2016, the college said, 'We will be forever grateful to General Sam for his service to Hampden-Sydney and to this nation. We will all miss his stories, counsel and kindness. But we also know that General Sam's legacy and character live on in the foundation of this college, and in the countless individuals worldwide he inspired to service and taught to lead.'

Much has been written about leadership and what separates a great leader from a poor one. Brigadier General Frank Merrill was the latter because he had little integrity; he took the credit for the courage of others and blamed others when the fault was his own.

In contrast, Colonel Cary Owtram commanded the immense respect of the men with whom he was imprisoned at Chungkai from where Allied prisoners of the Japanese were put to work on building the Burma railway under the most appalling conditions. Owtram, the British camp commandant, died in 1993 having revealed little of his experience to his children. They learned something of the character of their father from a letter published in the *Lancaster Guardian* on 15 January that year: 'On many occasions, I witnessed his receiving brutal beatings for his adamant and steadfast refusals to order sick men out on the railway,' wrote a Mr AB Miller. 'This occurred on so many occasions that eventually even the Japanese accepted the fact that if Cary Owtram said so, then those men were indeed too sick to work. There are many ex-POWs, including myself, who owe their survival to Colonel Owtram.'

Colonel Guy Prendergast, who commanded the LRDG from 1941–43, was also a leader who inspired others through the strength of his scrupulous character. He was an austere man, but a fair one, who understood the complexity of human nature, especially in the crucible of combat.

As an astute judge of character, Prendergast had a trenchant idea of the qualities required to thrive in a special forces unit such as the LRDG. In a recruitment drive in 1943, he listed the essential characteristics for any new recruit:

A. *Tact, initiative, and a keen understanding of his fellow men;*

B. *Intelligence above the average, and a sound military background;*

C. *Courage and endurance;*

D. *Perfect physical condition;*

E. *A readiness to undertake any task that might be required of him;*

F. *Some technical or language qualification.*

G. *Youthfulness – few men over the age of thirty [will be] accepted.*

But for potential officers, there was an additional requirement: he must possess a 'knowledge of men' because 'for days on end, he would have to live with his men, endure their hardships, share their disappointments, and rejoice in their success,' stated Prendergast. 'Not only did he need to know more about their job than they knew themselves, but he also had to be more expert than they in handling weapons and equipment.'

War is unique in its capacity to test a person's integrity. Charles Wilson, Lord Moran, a medical officer in the First World War on the Western Front, and personal physician to Winston Churchill during the Second, wrote in his book, *The Anatomy of Courage*, that 'Man's acts in war are dictated not by courage, nor by fear, but by conscience, of which war is the final test.'

* * *

The Second World War was different to the First in that civilians also had their character tested in the most challenging of circumstances, and the results could be surprising. Langdon Gilkey was a twenty-four-year-old American teacher in China when he and 2,000 other Western civilians were interned by the Japanese in 1943 in a camp in Shantung Province. 'The most important lesson I learned is that there are no cut-and-dried categories in human life,' he said of his two years of imprisonment. 'Over and over, "respectable people" – one of the commonest labels applied in social intercourse – turned out to be unco-operative, irritable and, worse, dishonest. Conversely, many who were neither "respectable" nor pious, were, in fact, valiant.'

Into that second category fell a young Englishwoman called Clair Richards. She was regarded as a woman of low morals initially. There were 'stories of a lurid past in Peking', stories that her tight skirts and low-cut blouses encouraged. 'It is safe to say that when she swung into view, the words "character" and "moral" were not the first to pop into the minds of the envious, horrified or interested observer,' wrote Gilkey.

But Clair proved herself a woman of immense industry and integrity when she volunteered to supervise the women's kitchen. Hygiene had been declining for months and pilfering from the stores had become commonplace, depleting an already meagre supply of food. Clair, with a mix of humour, hard work and 'rugged and undeviating honesty', transformed the kitchen. 'Looked upon by most of the pious as so wicked they were embarrassed to be seen talking with her, she had, in fact, a higher moral character than they did,' reflected Gilkey.

There were millions of young women like Clair in Britain during the Blitz. Many put their integrity to good use as Land Girls, firewomen, nurses or air-raid wardens. Others displayed their courage and integrity when they were alone and frightened. During the heaviest and most destructive night of the London Blitz, 10–11 May 1941, twenty-nine-year-old Olivia Smith was asleep in her Maida Vale home when she was woken by a 'loud howling whistle from a falling firebomb'. Peering out of the window, Smith saw that the incendiary bomb had dropped in her neighbour's garden. 'I ran out,' she wrote in her diary, 'and with some difficulty pulled myself over the wall by means of the branch of an elder tree at the bottom of the garden and ran to deal with it barehanded . . . just as I was getting through the last stages of my job, a tremendous outburst of noise thundered from the sky. I ran like a hare to the wall . . . for what seemed like hours

I dithered and fumbled on the wall top, clawing frantically at the twigs that enlaced me and caught in my clothes.'

Why did Olivia do what she did? She could have got back into bed, pulled the quilt over her head and told herself that the bomb was not her responsibility. But she ran out in the middle of an air raid to douse the incendiary for the same reason that Porter Jarrell burrowed into a collapsed building: they were of people of strong moral character.

* * *

One of the buzzwords of recent years is 'post-truth'; in Britain, America and most of the West, it's claimed by commentators from across the political spectrum that this is a post-truth era. The more accurate description is 'post-integrity'.

Contrast Olivia Smith's actions with those of two Police Community Support Officers (PCSOs) who, in 2007, did not enter a lake in Greater Manchester where a ten-year-old boy was drowning. Their senior officer, DCI Phil Owen, excused their passivity because the police 'regularly warn the public of the dangers of going into unknown stretches of water, so it would have been inappropriate for PCSOs, who are not trained in water rescue, to enter the pond.'

This was not an isolated incident. In 2008, a woman fell into a disused mineshaft in Scotland while taking a shortcut home; firefighters were quickly on the scene but an inquest later heard that those who volunteered to enter the mineshaft were overruled by senior officers 'for health and safety reasons'. In 2015, a seventeen-year-old drowned in an east London canal as two policemen watched from the towpath and a police helicopter filmed his desperate struggle. Asked at the inquest why the police only entered the canal four minutes after the teenager had disappeared underwater, the officer in charge said they had to carry out a 'dynamic assessment' of potential risks before going in.

As Lord Moran wrote, 'man's acts in war are dictated not by courage, nor by fear, but by conscience, of which war is the final test.' But sometimes war isn't needed to test a man's character; a simple emergency will do, and too often in recent years in Britain, the test has been failed because health and safety has been put before humanity.

Of course, there are many members of the emergency services who have displayed the utmost courage and integrity in the line of duty, such as PC Charlie Guenigault, who was off-duty on the night three Islamist terrorists attacked people on London Bridge in June 2017. Despite being unarmed, he ran towards the men and was badly wounded as he tried to protect the public. Three years later, another unarmed and off-duty police officer apprehended a knifeman in Reading as he carried out a deadly attack.

Significantly, on both occasions, these brave young men acted instinctively and of their own accord. But one wonders if their actions might have been thwarted had a box-ticking senior officer been present.

Britain is still, by and large, a 'have-a-go' nation, a country where people are likely to step in and help out rather than walk on by. That was certainly the case in November 2019 when members of the public battled another Islamist terrorist on London Bridge. But if the British public can be counted on to do the right thing, the same isn't true of the – and I use the term loosely – 'great and the good'. Increasingly in the twenty-first century, people in positions of authority are – how can one put this diplomatically? – 'integrity-lite'.

Think of the number of high-profile figures – from politicians to city mayors to Government advisers to eminent scientists to chief medical officers – who flouted the lockdown rules during the COVID-19 pandemic. Most were forced to resign – except for a certain Mr Cummings, the PM's chief adviser – but their actions reinforced the impression among the public at large that the great and the good believe there is one rule for them and another for the little people.

'This is part of a pattern of duplicity in public life,' wrote Matthew Syed in *The Sunday Times* when discussing the subject. He then listed several examples of sharp practice down the years: of Thatcherite ministers who were employed in the industries they privatised, of New Labour ministers offering to use their access to promote private interests for £3,000 a day and regulators who say they are serving public interest, but 'who draft complex rules so that they can later gain lucrative jobs in the private sector interpreting them'.

A lack of integrity among the élite is nothing new, of course, as 2020's BBC dramatisation of the Profumo affair demonstrated. What's new is the shamelessness.

John Profumo resigned as Secretary of State for War in 1963 and, to atone for his sins, devoted the rest of his life to working as a volunteer for a charity to alleviate poverty. How passé. In recent years, Neil Hamilton, Peter Mandelson, Denis MacShane and Chris Huhne have all disgraced their office but they remained in the public eye, carving out new careers as highly-paid consultants, celebrities or journalists.

But when it comes to shameless MPs, no one can hold a match to happily-married Keith Vaz, who was filmed in the company of male prostitutes in 2016, boasting he would pay for cocaine; not only did Vaz remain in his post, but the following month he was appointed to the Justice Select Committee. This, incidentally, was the same Vaz who, in 2002, was suspended from the House of Commons for one month after the Standards Committee declared he has 'failed in his duty under the code of conduct to act on all occasions in accordance with the public trust placed in him'.

In 2012, Essex University published a report warning that Britain was facing an 'integrity crisis' because of a toleration of 'low-level dishonesty'. When one of the report's authors, Professor Paul Whiteley, appeared on *BBC Breakfast*, he was asked to account for the decline in the nation's integrity. 'We think it is because their role models are not very good – footballers who cheat on their wives, journalists who hack people's phones. Gradually, people are tending to become more dishonest, they are more willing to tell lies, more willing to tolerate adultery. It's slow over time and going on in the background, but pretty evidentially there.'

Whiteley could also have mentioned the 2009 parliamentary expenses scandal or the 'dodgy dossier' of 2002 infamy, which propelled Britain to war against Iraq on the bogus claim that Saddam Hussein had weapons of mass destruction that were ready to launch in forty-five minutes.

* * *

Contrary to the lurid claims of the Tory MP Simon Wingfield-Digby in 1944, the SBS were not a band of 'murderous, renegade cut-throats'. The American war correspondent Donald Grant came to know them well during the Aegean campaign and, in one radio broadcast in May 1944, described his encounter with a section, among whom was Porter Jarrell. '[Jarrell] told me that these soldiers are the best bunch of fighting men in the world,' said Grant. Furthermore, unlike their Nazi foe, 'they have kept their sense of decency and honour'.

The previous autumn, Grant had gone on patrol with Dick Holmes' unit, and from him learned of the story of Heinz and Ulrich. The two Germans had strayed into the SBS hideout as they waited to be evacuated by motor launch after raiding a Cretan airfield. There was a brief discussion as to what should be done with them. No one fancied shooting them in cold blood, so the SBS took the pair with them back across the Mediterranean to Mersa Matruh and from there in a truck to Cairo.

Dick and his SBS mates grew to like Heinz and Ulrich and so, before handing them over for interrogation in the Egyptian capital, the SBS treated them to as much ice cream as they could eat in Cairo's most prestigious café. The top brass were furious when they got wind of the incident and demanded an explanation from the SBS. 'We treated them as normal human beings,' replied the officer in charge, David Sutherland. 'You must appreciate that we in the SBS, due to our role, have a different code of conduct in these matters.'

9

Duty

Duty defined Bob Lowson's life. Duty to his country and to his family and friends. Yet Bob wasn't a stiff ex-serviceman with a blind devotion to Britain.

Apart from SAS regimental reunions, where he could catch up with old pals over a pint or two, he avoided military occasions because he found all the pomp and ceremony oppressive. He was opposed to the invasion of Iraq in 2003 because he considered the reason for going to war spurious.

When Bob went off to war in 1939, he was just a kid, not yet nineteen. His dad was a sailor. During the Great War, he had been torpedoed twice. He was, remembered Bob, 'a real hard case', a remote man who rarely talked to his son.

On the day Bob was called up, his dad walked into his

bedroom and, for the first time in his life, 'he sounded like a human being'. First he gave his son his cherished watch, then he offered some advice. No need to be a hero, just do your duty. And you're going to be among men now so don't tell lies and don't bear grudges. 'The best advice I ever had,' Bob reflected more than six decades later. 'I've tried to live up to that.'

Few British soldiers saw more combat than Bob in the Second World War. He first engaged the Germans in combat in Norway in April 1940 serving with the Independent Companies, and in the five following years he exchanged fire with them in North Africa, Sicily, Italy, France, Belgium and Germany. His war ended in April 1945 when, by now a decorated sergeant in the SAS, he was shot in the thigh by a sniper in a German forest. His squadron commander believed him dead but two of Bob's pals, Doug Arnold and Billy Stalker, sprinted across a pasture and dragged Bob from a ditch full of water.

Bob spent months in Manchester Royal Infirmary, tended by a nurse called Myfanwy, the fiancée of Doug Arnold. In the last years of his life, Bob would drive to north Wales to take the widowed Myfanwy out for lunch as a 'thank you' for what she had done for him sixty years earlier.

Bob's wife had died a few years earlier. It hadn't been a happy marriage, he told me. They had met in 1937, at a school of dancing, and wed in 1945 but, by the 1950s, it was apparent his wife was mentally ill. Bob, a talented sportsman pre-war who was troubled by the wound to his leg for the rest of his life, consulted various medical experts, but none was much good. When he told one female doctor that his wife was 'dreadfully difficult to live with', the GP shot back with a sardonic smile, 'Aren't we all?' He was advised to commit his wife to an institution but, after visiting a couple, Bob dismissed the idea. 'They were horrible places, madhouses back then. I couldn't abandon her.'

So Bob built an annexe on their bungalow for his wife and, for years, they lived separate lives. They had only one ritual – early each evening, his wife would appear in the sitting room and play the piano while Bob drank a sherry. Then one night, when they were in their late seventies, Bob's wife knocked on his door as he was preparing for bed and said she didn't feel very well. Could she lie next to him? She was still poorly the next morning so Bob went to the chemist. When he returned, she was dead.

My friendship with Bob began a few years later, when I began researching a book about the wartime SAS. We first met in October 2002 in the bar of the Adelphi Hotel in Liverpool. Bob had initially been reluctant to meet. As he told me, 'There's a lot of shit been written about the SAS.' He had one example with him, a previous book about the regiment's exploits in the Second World War. He had marked half-a-dozen inaccuracies. 'I know that wasn't how it was because I was bloody well there!'

Despite our fifty-year age gap, we became friends. I stayed with him on several occasions and I reciprocated the hospitality. On the eve of my wedding, Bob sent me and my wife-to-be a cheque; the following year, he presented our daughter with a silver spoon. We corresponded regularly before his death in 2013. In the letter I treasure most, he said that he enjoyed our association because it had boosted his self-esteem. I had coaxed out of this humble and dutiful man a realisation. 'I'd always considered I didn't do much in the war,' he wrote. 'But talking to you, I realise I did do more than I thought.'

'His generation are a class act,' I wrote in my diary on receiving Bob's letter, 'so superior to the braggarts of the post-1960s.'

I've never met a member of Bob's generation who bragged. They all saw their war service as 'doing their duty'. Yet this generation did not have their parents' naïveté; they went to war with their eyes open. There was no widespread belief that it 'would be over by Christmas', as there had been in 1914; neither was there the blind obedience to the flag. On the contrary, there was often a robust cynicism inherited from their fathers, whose unconditional patriotism had been blown to smithereens on the Somme or at Ypres.

The generational wars of the early twenty-first century are nothing new. For 'OK Boomer' in 2020, read 'OK Victorian' in 1939. The ruling class, born in the nineteenth century, regarded Bob's generation as soft and decadent, while they looked on their elders as relics from another age. It was the Italian leader, Benito Mussolini, who perhaps best summed up Britain in this period when, after hosting Neville Chamberlain and Lord Halifax to dinner in January 1939, he said of his guests they 'are not made of the same stuff as Francis Drake and the other magnificent adventurers who created the Empire. They are, after all, the tired sons of a long line of rich men . . . the British do not want to fight.'

Il Duce was right – the British didn't want a fight. But he didn't understand the national character – that they would fight if they had to. Not from the sort of thrusting patriotism that Mussolini embodied, but from a sense of duty.

And yet what made the British soldier unique among other armies of the Second World War was his lack of gung-ho enthusiasm. Other powers were inspired or intimidated into action by emperors and tyrants or, in the case of the Dominions and America, a desire to show the world what their young country could do; but the British trudged off to war wearily. 'Grumbling is the life blood of the British soldier,' wrote one of Lowson's comrades in the SAS, Captain Malcolm Pleydell, their medical officer in 1942. Specifically, during the war in North Africa, it was noted by the British soldier that they were paid less than any Dominion soldier. 'The British are always putting up with far more for far less than anybody else,' wrote Pleydell. 'There is only one thing we could do and that would be to strike. But that would be unjust to others. Our conscience would not allow it . . . we prefer to submit to wrongs and grumble over them, than to alter them and feel that we may be doing the country a disservice.'

It was the conscience of the Greatest Generation that made them so supreme. Like Bob Lowson, many of their fathers and uncles had fought in the Great War. Those who survived returned home physically or psychologically damaged; their experiences spawned a new genre of literature in the 1920s and 1930s, the anti-war memoir. One consequence was that, in 1933, the Oxford Union Society passed the motion in a debate that 'This House will under no circumstances fight for its King and country'.

Britain was shocked but *The Times* reminded its readers in an acidic leader entitled 'Children's Hour' that the students who passed the motion were a 'little clique of cranks', and not representative of British youth. They, fortunately, were not wallowing in what the paper called 'universal decadence'.

The *Times'* analysis was correct. Six years later, the country's young went off to fight. Jim Booth was representative of many upper-middle-class young men in 1939. His father had fought in the Great War and been left 'pretty shattered by it all'. Jim was educated at Eton and, in September 1939, went up to Cambridge to read Natural Science. 'I couldn't stand it during the first term, I felt constrained by the fact all my friends were in the services,' he explained. 'Eventually, I said, "Bugger this", and joined up.'

Another SAS veteran whom I interviewed, Bill Deakins, subtitled his war memoir 'Sod this for a game of soldiers'. He didn't want to leave his home in Torbay to fight, much less kill another man, but he knew it was his duty. 'I had no feelings or thoughts of going off to kill people,' he said. 'The personal side did not come into it . . . but the belief that in some small way I could do my bit to bring the world back to some sort of sanity.'

The desire to 'do their bit', the Greatest Generation's euphemism for 'do their duty', which felt a little pretentious to most, extended from the rich and famous to the lowliest Londoner, like Iris Croker, who was sixteen and a student at Woolwich Polytechnic in 1939. She was one of 1.5 million Britons who volunteered for the Civil Defence, in her case performing shifts as a firewatcher during air raids. 'We had to take it in turns to stay upstairs in Boots [the chemist] where there were some bunks that we could lie on if we had the chance,' she recalled. 'The idea was that, if incendiary bombs were dropped, we were expected to put the fires out using stirrup pumps.'

The actor David Niven returned from Hollywood to enlist in the Rifle Brigade, ignoring the advice of Britain's ambassador to the USA who suggested that he could best serve his country 'on the screen'; another actor, Michael Redgrave, joined the Royal Navy as an ordinary seaman. His friend Noel Coward took him out for lunch in Plymouth on 10 July 1941 and wrote in his diary that he found Redgrave 'Extremely healthy and happy . . . having left a luxurious film star life to be an ordinary seaman, he is obviously having a wonderful time'.

Arguably nothing in the Second World War symbolised the nation's sense of duty more than the 'miracle of Dunkirk' in May 1940 when an armada of naval ships and civilian boats evacuated 330,000 British and French troops from the beach at Dunkirk from under the noses of the Germans. 'Fishermen, yachtsmen, yacht builders, yacht clubs, river boatmen, and boat-building and hiring firms manned their craft with volunteer crews and rushed them to the assembly point, although they did not then know for what purpose they were required,' said the Admiralty in a communiqué following the evacuation. 'They operated successfully by day and night under the most difficult and dangerous conditions. The Admiralty cannot speak too highly of the services of all concerned. They were essential to the success of the operation and the means of saving thousands of lives . . . they showed magnificent and tireless spirit.'

In his 1941 essay 'The Lion and the Unicorn: Socialism and the English Genius', George Orwell wrote that Dunkirk was the turning point of the war for the British people. 'After eight months of vaguely wondering what the war was about, the people suddenly knew what they had to do,' he wrote. 'It was like the awakening of a giant.'

The reason for the initial sluggishness, suggested Orwell, was that 'in the working class, patriotism is profound but it is unconscious. The working man's heart does not leap when he sees a Union Jack . . . the patriotism of the common people is not vocal or even conscious'.

In the same year that Orwell wrote his essay about Dunkirk, the pacifist feminist author Vera Brittain described her love of country in *England's Hour*. Her patriotism wasn't the flag, the Royal Family, the buildings or the Government; rather it was the 'tolerant endurance of British men and women . . . their patient amusement in Hyde Park or on Tower Hill when open-air orators proclaim opinions on which they are diametrically opposed . . . their brave, grumbling stoicism in danger and adversity . . . their staunch refusal even in maximum peril to become panic-stricken. But more than all, England for me means the fields and lanes of its lovely countryside . . . the misty, soft-edged horizon which is the superb gift to the eyes of this fog-laden island.'

John Colville, a young member of Winston Churchill's inner circle in 1940, witnessed this tolerance on 27 April of that year while in a pub in Leicester Square. 'A group of bespectacled intellectuals remained firmly seated while "God Save the King" was played,' he wrote in his diary. 'Everybody looked but nobody did anything, which shows that the war has not yet made us lose our sense of proportion or become noisily jingoistic.'

Ironically, the tolerance of the majority was not reciprocated by a minority of the left-wing intelligentsia, some of whom were in the 'little clique of cranks' who voted in the Oxford Union debate in 1933. As Orwell explained in his essay, these people 'felt that there is something slightly disgraceful in being an Englishman and that it is a duty to snigger at every English institution'. Furthermore, what united the left-wing intelligentsia was 'their severance from the common culture of the country'. They considered that they had no obligation to their country. Indeed, they were ashamed by it, and particularly its people, and had no intention of doing their duty. Some actively worked against it, of course – the Cambridge students, for example, who spied for Stalin's murderous Soviet Union.

This sentiment of national shame has become mainstream on the left during the last fifty years and now millions, to paraphrase Orwell, would consider stealing a charity box less iniquitous than standing to attention during the national anthem.

The British flag, and more specifically, England's Cross of

St George, has become a source of shame and ridicule, to the extent that a senior Labour politician, Emily Thornberry, publicly sneered at a man for flying his flag from his house. The then-Shadow Attorney General apologised for her gesture but it wasn't enough to save her place on the front bench. In 2015 it was revealed that Labour's general election candidate in Ceredigion had once said that people who displayed St George's flags were 'simpletons' and 'casual racists'.

Patriotism has become a pejorative term; during the COVID-19 pandemic, one Oxford University lecturer, Dr Emily Cousens, penned an article expressing the hope that Oxford didn't contribute to eliminating the disease. 'If my university is the first to develop the vaccine, I'm worried that it will be used as it has been in the past, to fulfil its political, patriotic function as proof of British excellence,' wrote Dr Cousens, 'that being white, male and Oxford-educated may not be the only criteria for effective leadership'.

If a people aren't patriotic, then why should they have a duty to their country and their fellow beings? If one is told repeatedly that the British flag is a racist symbol of a country with a deeply shameful past, then why should we be surprised that young Britons climb on to the Cenotaph and attempt to set fire to the Union flag? If the erstwhile Shadow Chancellor, John McDonnell, labels Winston Churchill a 'villain", and a member of the Scottish Parliament describes him as a 'mass murderer', then mobs of immature youths will, of course, try to demolish his statue in Parliament Square or, failing that, deface it with insults.

We have reached this sorry point because history is now superficially taught in most schools; indeed, thousands of young people appear to get their historical knowledge from that well-known bastion of intellectualism – social media. As a result, there are excruciating moments of ignorance, such as the one on *Channel Four News* in June when a community leader in London was asked her opinion of Churchill. 'I've heard many arguments on both sides,' replied the woman, who is also an Independent Police Advisory Group Chair. 'Some say that he's a racist. Some say that he's a hero. I haven't personally met him.'

And there's little use in looking to higher education for historical help because that's long since been in the control of the far-left, and its modus operandi is to denigrate British history and portray the past in the worst possible light. And not just the past.

To listen to some people in the mainstream and social media, one would believe Britain is a hateful and intolerant hellhole for anyone who is not of John Bull stock. Yet time after time, studies from respected institutions reveal otherwise; such as the YouGov–Cambridge Globalism survey in May 2019, which, as the *Guardian* reported, found that 'British people are more persuaded of the benefits of immigration than any other major European nation'.

Three months earlier, the *Frontiers in Sociology* journal had published the findings of a study in European attitudes towards racism and religious intolerance in which Britain was described as one of the least racist nations on the continent. 'Prejudice against immigrant workers or minority ethnic and religious groups is rare in the UK, perhaps even slightly rarer than in equivalently developed EU countries,' said the study co-author Professor Mariah Evans, of the University of Nevada.

But the political class is so scared of standing up for British history, so unable to grasp the difference between quiet patriotism and angry nationalism that, instead of sticking up for Churchill and pointing out he had more virtues than flaws, they board him up. Surely a new low was reached in bitter irony in June 2020 when President Emmanuel Macron bestowed on London the Légion d'honneur for its courage and resilience eighty years earlier. Yet hours before the French president arrived in the capital, Churchill's statue had been hidden for fear he might provoke unrest.

These incidents are the fruition of a warning sounded in 2010 by the eminent historian Simon Schama, when he said that the way history was taught was creating a two-tier Britain, a tier who 'grow up with a sense of our shared memory as a living, urgently present body of knowledge', and a tier 'who have been encouraged to treat it as little more than ornamental polishing'.

In June 2020, we saw a group of young soldiers doing a bit of ornamental scrubbing on the plinth of Earl Haig's statue in Whitehall after it had been vandalised by left-wing agitators. A group of young women mocked them as they cleaned the graffiti from 'your precious memorial'. Their choice of words was instructive; not 'our' memorial, but 'yours'; Schama's two-tier Britain writ large.

In a speech in 2018, General Sir Nick Carter, the head of Britain's armed forces, expressed his concern that young Britons no longer had a sense of duty. 'I think my generation understand the notion of service all too well, naturally recognising that freedom, without the commitment to service, without charity, duty or pride in one's country, is unworthy of our British values,' he said.

The general was generalising, unwittingly referencing the two-tier Britain that Simon Schama had described. Many young Britons have no sense of civic duty, but an equal number are deeply patriotic, not in a chest-thumping, flag-waving way, but doing their bit to help in a national emergency.

Think of the thousands of young volunteers for the NHS scheme, and also the many young Brits who answered the call for fruit- and vegetable-pickers. The 'Pick for Britain' campaign was launched at the start of the lockdown, when it was feared that tons of fruit would rot because foreign workers – the normal fruit-pickers – were unable to fly in. One fruit firm in Cambridgeshire hailed the 'legendary' response of Britons – from across the age and social spectrum – to the Pick for Britain scheme. One young volunteer, a student called Martha, admitted it had been hard going at first. 'I was tired at the end of my first day,' she told the *Daily Express*. 'I was exhausted a lot more than I thought I'd be – but that's a positive. It's nice after spending weeks alone not doing anything.'

Martha and the other young fruit pickers are little different to the Land Girls of the Second World War. 'It takes guts to be a Land Girl,' declared Lady Denman, the Land Army's honorary director, at a recruitment rally in March 1941. In reporting her Ladyship's words, the *Chichester Observer* remarked: 'The girls who have slid to work at 5.30am on the dark mornings during the frosts of the last two winters and worked long hours in the summer heat to bring in the hay and the harvest cannot be accused of being unwilling to take on any job that comes.'

Her Majesty the Queen did her bit in the war as a teenage member of the Auxiliary Territorial Service, and she's fulfilled her duty to the nation ever since. She was arguably the only high-profile figure throughout Britain's chaotic response to COVID-19 to act with dignity, appearing on our television screens to remind us of where our duty lay. 'Together we are tackling this disease, and I want to reassure you that if we remain united and resolute, then we will overcome it,' she said in her address to the nation. 'I hope in the years to come, everyone will be able to take pride in how they responded to this challenge, and . . . the pride in who we are is not a part of our past, it defines our present and our future.'

When she turned twenty-one in 1947, the then Princess Elizabeth made a speech in which she said, 'It is very simple. I declare before you all that my whole life, whether it be long or short, shall be devoted to your service.'

Since her accession to the throne in 1952, she has remained true to that declaration. 'Elizabeth's guiding philosophy has always been: "It's not about me",' wrote Deborah Orr in the *Guardian* in 2015, when the Queen became Britain's longest-reigning monarch. 'It's easy to see now that Diana, who believed for a time (understandably) that it was *all* about her, came closer to delivering the Queen's anathema – royalty as a part of celebrity culture – than anyone is likely to try for many decades to come.'

How could Orr have known that, just a few years later, Diana's youngest son, Harry, would try to copy his mother by blending royalty with celebrity culture. He was also unsuccessful. During the COVID-19 crisis, Harry provided a striking contrast to his dutiful grandmother as he fled to a Los Angeles mansion.

When I attended Bob Lowson's funeral in Birkenhead in 2013, I sensed the vicar was a little uncomfortable describing his remarkable war record. She told the congregation that he had been awarded a Distinguished Conduct Medal when, in fact, it was a Military Medal, one down in the hierarchy of gallantry medals. The gaffe would have tickled Bob.

He didn't go to war in search of medals or glory or out of any strong ideology. He loathed militarism as much as he did the bureaucrats at the Ministry of Pensions who had tried to cheat him out of his disability pension in 1946. Patriotism for Bob meant duty to his country, warts and all, and his coffin was draped with a Union flag because he was proud to have done his duty.

10

Self-Discipline

I met a couple of heroes on 17 August 2004. The morning was spent in the company of Harry Beckingham at his home in Southport, and in the afternoon I visited John Freeborn in the same town.

Beckingham had been a bomb disposal officer during the war and Freeborn a fighter pilot. The survival rates of their professions weren't high, but one trait brought the pair through unscathed – self-discipline.

They had it in spades, although neither was the ramrod-straight military stereotype. 'Harry,' I wrote in my diary, 'is a bit of a boy', by which I meant he knew how to enjoy life. 'A nice man,' I added, 'and either a very brave one or somehow he was able to suppress his anxiety'.

As for John, whom I'd visited earlier in the year, he was

'as refreshingly cantankerous as ever . . . and over a couple of pints in the pub we put the world to rights'.

Sixty-five years earlier, in August 1939, the eighteen-year-old Harry was preparing to go to Manchester University to study Structural Engineering. Life had other plans. He had joined a territorial unit of Royal Engineers in June that year and, when war was declared, he became a full-time sapper. In March 1940, he made the elementary military mistake of volunteering for a new assignment, he told me, and, as a consequence, he was posted to Sheffield to study the science of bomb disposal. He and his small band of fellow volunteers were told that there wouldn't be much to defusing the German bombs. 'They would always be lying on the surface . . . that was the theory,' explained Harry.

When the Blitz started and Harry was posted to London, he discovered that there was a little more to it than that. 'The trouble with London,' he told me, his lip curling with northern contempt, 'is that it's all basically built on blue clay, so bombs slid down to depths of 20ft or more.'

Over lunch, Harry described one of his first jobs. 'A stick of unexploded bombs landed in a cemetery in Leytonstone, so we had to start digging them up,' he said. 'The bodies were stinking to high heaven and the only way we could kill the stench was to pour creosote round the holes. We removed the bodies with shovels, but they disintegrated as soon as they hit the air. We put them to one side, got down into the ground to defuse the bombs, and then shovelled them back in afterwards.'

For nearly two months, Harry's company defused bombs. They worked from 8.00am to 8.00pm, stopping only when it was too dark to see what they were defusing. 'We got up in the morning, had breakfast, climbed into the three-tonner and went off to a job,' he said. 'I can't ever remember being worried, but I was young.'

The average life-expectancy of a bomb disposal officer in the first weeks of the Blitz was ten weeks; nine were killed in the week ending 21 September, and twenty-one in the week ending 12 October. Not only were the bombs deep inside the blue clay of the capital, but they came fitted with ever more elaborate fuses, one of which, the Number 17, had a maximum time delay of seventy-two hours. Then there was the Number 50 fuse, an anti-handling fuse, whose trembler switch could be activated by the smallest of vibrations, like a lorry's engine at the end of the street.

On the morning of 11 May 1941 (the last heavy raid of the Blitz), Harry's company was called from its base in Chelsea to defuse a 250kg unexploded bomb that had fallen on Platform 10 of Victoria Station. First, they cut the sleepers on the tracks; next they cleared away the ballast from the edges and then they chipped away at the hole with pick-axes and shovels. They often nattered as they worked, seeking comfort in camaraderie. 'Digging was always the hairiest part of the job because the reason a bomb hadn't exploded was usually because it had been dropped too low from the aircraft to allow time for the charge to pass through the resistor into the firing capacitor,' he said. 'So it hit the ground inert instead of being fully charged. But there was still energy in the bomb and vibrations from people digging might well make it come alive.'

How did he keep such thoughts from his mind, I asked Harry. He laughed and replied, 'Too much thinking was unhealthy. I just kept to my philosophy that, if a bomb went off and I was right on top of it, then I wouldn't know anything about it. It would be a nice quick death.'

John Freeborn saw several of his friends die in the Battle of Britain and, often, the end wasn't quick. What every fighter pilot feared was a 'flamer', trapped in a burning cockpit. The spectre 'frightened the hell' out of John and, in one dogfight in July 1940, the top tank of his Spitfire was hit by cannon fire. Had the tank not been full, the vapour would probably have exploded; as it was, John nursed his aircraft back to base, remembering everything he had been taught in training about what to do in such a situation.

In his Spitfire, John flew more operational hours in the Battle of Britain than any other RAF pilot. He shot down thirteen enemy aircraft and was credited with twelve 'probables', for which he was awarded a Distinguished Flying Cross.

John and Harry both mentioned 'luck' when I asked why they thought they'd survived. There was an element of that, particularly when it came to defusing bombs. But paramount to their survival was their self-discipline. 'Practising all the time,' replied John, when I asked him what made an 'ace' fighter pilot. 'But I could never get blokes to do it. I would say "Get in the air!" and they would say, "I don't want to." But I did. I flew all the time.' This gave him a confidence in combat – so much so that, in a dogfight with a German, he would 'always come out on top'.

It was the same with Dick Holmes, MM, who fought for three years with the SBS. When I asked him what made a good special forces soldier, he replied, 'I told myself I was fighting men who hadn't done the training I had. They hadn't jumped out of aeroplanes or marched for miles on end. In my mind, I was better than them and that gave me – and I think the rest of the boys – a tremendous advantage when we went on a scheme. We were superior not only physically, but psychologically.'

Neither Dick nor John were disciplinarians in the military sense; John, in particular, ran into trouble on more than one occasion for pushing back against rules he considered ridiculous, a knack he'd developed at school in Yorkshire. To his dying day, he loathed bullying authoritarians. But his parents had instilled in him a self-discipline – to strive to be the best at whatever he chose to do. That meant listening to others who had more experience and knowledge and practising to become even better. But as he told his biographer, mastery of the self was the 'cornerstone of the principles' by which John led his life. 'Discipline teaches everybody the rights and wrongs of this world . . . you must never let the standards that are established slip.'

* * *

Ten years later, on a Sunday in the spring of 2014, I visited Jim Patch at his home in an isolated corner of Kent. As a non-driver, I cadged a lift off my mum and it required a combined effort in our navigational skills to locate Jim's house at the bottom of a winding country lane. He was outside waiting for us, immaculate in blazer and tie. My mum assumed he'd just returned from church or had a lunch appointment, but he hadn't; Jim was always well turned out, a habit he'd acquired in the war. Ditto Colonel Tom Moore.

Sewn on to the breast pocket of Jim's blazer was a scorpion inside a wheel, the regimental badge of the LRDG, the pioneers of British special forces warfare, whose contribution to the winning of the war in North Africa was acknowledged by General Bernard Montgomery.

If Jim had been born half a century later, he might well have been a computer geek; as it was, the Londoner had an interest in radios as a youngster and, when he was called up in May 1940, he trained as a wireless operator. Jim wasn't a bayonet-and-bravado soldier; he was erudite, gentle and softly spoken, and possessed of an iron self-discipline. 'I was highly delighted to be with the LRDG, because clearly one was given a lot of individual initiative and freedom and the normal military discipline was supplanted by a very strong self-discipline,' he said. 'We realised at once that, if we didn't pull our weight and do our job as supposed to, we would be out on our necks right away.'

Once a soldier was selected for the LRDG, the onus was on him to conduct himself in a manner worthy of such a unit. That entailed a discipline different to the regular army standards, which proved beyond a handful of recruits. 'Some of them were far too cheeky and they would realise that there was this lax – as you might say – military discipline, without obligatory saluting and standing to attention and polishing of boots and whitewashing of stones, and all the rest of it,' recalled Patch. 'Certain people would feel so free by this lack of discipline that they would start calling the commanding officer by his Christian name, and that kind of thing. They were sorted out at once and sent back.'

To be sent back to their regiment – Returned to Unit (RTU'd) in special forces jargon – was the ultimate shame for the LRDG. 'We were regarded as an undisciplined, wild rabble,' said Mike 'Lofty' Carr, one of Jim's pals in the LRDG. 'But we didn't think much of army discipline because the self-discipline that we needed in the LRDG was a lot more demanding, but anyone who didn't fit in, who didn't meet the LRDG etiquette, was gone.'

When he was in his late forties, Mike decided on a career change. Packing in car insurance, he trained as a teacher and ended his working life teaching art to sixth-form students. Later in life, Mike grew his hair long and cultivated a luxuriant beard, but it would be a stretch to call him an 'ageing hippy'. When I stayed with him and his wife, Barbara, at their home in the Wirral in 2014, I was in the company of a man at peace with the world. They took me to a local tapas bar for supper; it was about half a mile from their home and Lofty refused to take the car. He was determined to get there under his own steam, using his walking frame, which he did. Needless to say, he was smartly dressed, to boot.

Because of their training, and their self-discipline, Jim and Lofty became masters of their own destiny, as did Harry Beckingham and John Freeborn. They were taught to respect the enemy but, above all, to respect the environment; don't be afraid of it, but don't believe you've got the better of it. Man will never beat nature, but he can live in harmony with it, with the right mindset.

This was the premise of Freddie Spencer Chapman's memoir, *The Jungle is Neutral*, written in 1949. Freddie had waged a short-lived guerrilla campaign against the Japanese in 1942 but, when he ran out of explosives and comrades, he had spent more than two years in the Malayan jungle collecting intelligence and evading the Japanese, who were intent on hunting him down. That they didn't was because he was superior mentally and physically to his adversary.

'The human body is capable of bearing immense privation,' he had written after an expedition to the Arctic in the early 1930s. 'It is the state of mind that is important.'

In another extreme environment, the same rule applied to Freddie. Occasionally in the Malayan jungle he encountered stragglers from the British Army, few of whom survived long, which was true also of most Japanese soldiers who became lost. In explaining the reason for the title of his memoir, Chapman wrote of the jungle: 'It provides any amount of fresh water, and unlimited cover for friend as well as foe – an armed neutrality, if you like, but neutrality nevertheless. It is the attitude of mind that determines whether you go under or survive. There is nothing either good or bad, but thinking makes it so. The jungle is neutral.'

Entwined with self-discipline is self-control, the ability not only to perform your role efficiently but to do so with clarity and composure.

When I contacted Richard James in 2004 to request an interview to talk about his time flying with Guy Gibson, he was initially reluctant. Too much nonsense has been written about Gibson, he told me, or words to that effect. Eventually, he agreed to see me, however, and Richard enlightened me about the legendary Dambusters leader.

He and Gibson had flown together in 1941 in 29 Squadron, hunting German fighters in the night sky over Britain. Their Beaufighter was equipped with the secretive Airborne Interception, a radar system that picked out hostile aircraft. Sergeant James was its operator and it was his job to use AI to guide Gibson on to the target. 'Flying with Gibson was terrific,' Richard told me, 'because he was a first-class pilot. He could land a Beaufighter better than anyone in the squadron, even at night time . . . he also practised landing on one engine at night . . . and he was a very good instrument flyer and he used to tell me, "You've got to be able to take off entirely on instruments in this job."'

One night, in April 1941, Richard guided Gibson on to the tail of a Dornier bomber and the Beaufighter's cannons raked it with fire. 'We knew we hit it because pieces came off it, but the rear gunner fired back and this was the first time we'd received any return fire,' said James. 'To my surprise, Gibson turned away. That was the first time I realised Gibson had some fear, but he was just able to control it. When we landed, he wrote in the log book: "Returned fire, very accurate, quite frightening".'

Similar self-discipline, the mastery of one's fear, was frequently displayed on the home front. On 1 September 1939,

Mitzy Spooner metamorphosed from a young office worker to a member of the Auxiliary London Fire Service. Her HQ was in Dalston, east London, an area of the capital laid to waste during the Blitz. 'One night, an officer came round to us girls and asked if any of us could drive,' she recalled. 'I had learned to drive and had a licence but I had never driven anything other than the car I learned in.'

Mitzy stepped forward and, within a few minutes, was behind the wheel of a hose-laying lorry en route to a major fire as the bombs continued to drop. 'I felt really nervous,' she said. 'I said a little prayer and followed the convoy, hoping that I wouldn't go down a crater or let my side down. Was I pleased when the journey ended with me and the vehicle still in one piece!'

When Joan Wilson wrote to me, she admitted she was 'scared out of my life' during the Blitz. She was only twenty when she was sent in early 1941 to work cleaning guns in Woolwich Arsenal in what were unhelpfully dubbed the 'danger sheds'. 'We had our number painted on our backs in black paint,' she explained. 'We were told we must not run during a raid to the shelter because it would cause a panic. If you did run in a raid, you would be sacked.'

I also received a letter from Wendy Bishop, who wrote to tell me about life as a young nurse at RAF Wyton, a bomber base in Cambridgeshire. 'We went through some traumatic experiences – the sadness of our bombers who failed to return after a raid on Germany, or others who limped back home riddled with bullets,' she explained. 'We never heard of counselling. It was war, but my experience and discipline have held me in good stead over the years.'

Ditto Colonel Tom Moore. The discipline instilled in him during the Second World War when he served in the Duke of Wellington's Regiment and latterly the Royal Armoured Corps never left him; it's why he was able, at the age of 99 years and 11 months, to walk 10 laps of his 25m garden over 10 days. He subsequently fronted an army recruitment campaign in which the message was 'confidence lasts a lifetime'. So does self-discipline.

Colonel Tom captured the nation's imagination for more than just his walk. The Government labelled it a 'heroic effort' but there wasn't much 'heroism' in the old-fashioned sense of the word about his magnificent exploit.

We took Tom to our hearts because he was a reminder of the people we once were; immaculate in his regimental blazer and tie, his medals proudly on display, he exuded a stoic, modest, determined self-discipline. As a result, he inspired hundreds of Britons to embark upon their own challenges during the lockdown: from ninety-year-old Margaret Payne in Sutherland, Scotland, who raised approximately £350,000 by climbing the stairs of her house 300 times, a total distance of 731m (2,398ft), to six-year-old Frank Mills of Bristol, who overcame his spina bifida to walk 10m each day. Frank had hoped to raise £99 for charity – to match the age of Colonel Tom when he began his walk – but his bravery took the final figure to nearly £300,000.

Our political class could learn a thing or two from Colonel Tom and young Frank when it comes to self-discipline. It wasn't an edifying spectacle last year to see Jacob Rees-Mogg sprawled on a front bench during a debate or an MP physically trying to prevent the Speaker leaving the Chamber. So disorderly were the scenes last September during a Brexit debate that the BBC political correspondent Laura Kuenssberg likened them to a 'bear pit'.

As for dress, since 2017 politicians are no longer required to wear a tie in Parliament and it's now not uncommon to see MPs turning up to debates wearing football shirts or tracksuits. One of them, John Leech, boasted that he wore his sports kit because 'I was just bored of wearing a suit and it was a comfortable alternative'. The current Prime Minister is hardly a walking advertisement for sartorial elegance – even before barbers shut up shop for several months his hair was a law unto itself. Does wearing a tie or owning a comb really matter? Isn't it all rather old-fashioned? No. Self-discipline is perennial and its corollary is self-respect. Dress like a slob and you'll behave like one.

In the 1970s, David Stirling, the founder of the SAS, wrote an essay in which he explained its unparalleled success, which included the following: 'From the start, the SAS

Regiment has had some firmly held tenets from which we must never depart. They can be summarised as follows: (i) the unrelenting pursuit of excellence; ii) the maintaining of the highest standards of discipline in all aspects of the daily life of the SAS soldier, from the occasional precision drilling on the parade ground even to his personal turnout on leave.'

It's not hard to understand, therefore, why the SAS remains a force to be reckoned with . . . and Parliament does not.

11

Humour

O f all the Greatest Generation who I've met, none had such a charming laugh as Dame Vera Lynn. She was a 'youngster' when I had tea at her house in 2004, a mere eighty-seven, and I wrote in my diary that she was 'delightful: she still has a certain winsome, girlish quality about her and a lovely chuckle'.

We talked specifically about the Blitz, and her memories of performing in a variety show at the London Palladium called *Applesauce!* It was the most popular show in town in the spring of 1941, bringing together twenty-three-year-old Vera, the Forces' Sweetheart, Florence Desmond and her caustic impersonations of superstar actresses such as Marlene Dietrich and Greta Garbo, and the comedian Max Miller, legendary for his double entendres. The greybeards at the BBC considered Miller's risqué one-liners unworthy of Auntie, but the young servicemen and women roared with laughter at gags like 'Have you heard about the girl of eighteen who swallowed a pin, but didn't feel the prick until she was twenty-one?'

Vera still lived at home with her parents in Barking and drove to the Palladium each day in her pride and joy, a green canvas-roofed Austin. By early 1941, the worst of the Blitz was over; the raids were fewer but more ferocious. Still, theatres and cinemas across the country began to reopen in cities and there was no shortage of bums on seats. The people wanted entertaining; they wanted to laugh. As Vera wrote in her autobiography: 'Carrying on in the face of [raids] was seen as a small act of defiance. And maybe the public had grown fatalistic; if Hitler was going to drop a bomb on you, he might as well catch you having a laugh in the stalls as hiding under the stairs.'

There were a couple of big raids in April 1941 and, on both occasions, the wail of the air-raid siren silenced the stars. Some of the audience scurried away to seek shelter in one of the official refuges, but plenty hunkered down in their seats. 'Enough stayed for us to carry on with the show,' Vera told me. 'Then when the show had finished, we'd all have a little sing-song and some people would get up on stage and do a song of their own.'

Danger was a powerful stimulant, an aphrodisiac

for some, bringing an intensity and enjoyment to many young lives. Nancy Scott, who served in the Auxiliary Territorial Service in the war (multi-skilled, the ATS were employed as mechanics, searchlight operators, radar operators, telephonists, etc.), told me that she and her female colleagues had a whale of a time. 'I and the others were never in the least bit frightened. We were young and accepted the war and the bombing as completely natural. It was extraordinary. Theatres, dances and entertainment were in full swing, and we all enjoyed ourselves enormously.'

* * *

From time to time, I am asked to talk to schools, museums and at literary festivals about the wartime special forces. I often pitch a question to the audience: When the Special Air Service reformed in the 1950s, one of its senior officers, Major Dare Newell, picked the brains of several wartime special forces' officers. What, he enquired, were the personal traits he should look for when recruiting soldiers? From the answers, Newell produced seven essential characteristics for the SAS soldier: initiative, self-discipline, independence of mind, the ability to work without supervision, stamina, patience and . . . what?

That's the question I ask my audience – name the seventh characteristic? Only once have I received the right answer: a sense of humour.

That is not the man who has a fund of feeble mother-in-law jokes; on the contrary, show-offs, loudmouths and attention-seekers rarely make the grade. The humour was of another kind – the ability to find absurdity in adversity, to raise your face to the sky and laugh when plans go awry instead of dropping your head despondently.

'We pretty soon came to know one another's physical and mental capacities, and with them our own,' reflected John Verney, a wartime SBS officer. 'Strength and skill were respected, and a fair degree of both were essential, but everyone recognised that there were other qualities . . . on our type of operation, the man who could make you laugh was more worthwhile having than the bore who could shoot straight.'

Stephen Hastings, who served in the SAS in 1942, remarked in his war memoirs: 'He who laughs at life and lives with laughter is not just a boon to his friends, he is close to the gods.'

Anthony Greville-Bell was an upper-class SAS officer with a reputation as a ladies' man. Dashing and debonair, Tony, to the uninitiated, didn't appear the archetypal special forces officer but he possessed the seven precious characteristics, particularly an eye for the absurd. His first SAS operation was a disaster and he was lucky to escape with his life. 'You don't seethe against anyone, it's funny,' he told me. 'You just laugh about it and say, "What a bloody balls-up!" The thing about war is that you plan and plan, but the ones that win are the ones who are most able to overcome disasters, because nothing ever goes the way it's supposed to.'

One had to laugh in the Second World War because the alternative was self-pity, and that emotion was outlawed among the Greatest Generation. Millions experienced sorrow and suffered setbacks but, if self-pity did show, it was fleeting, a wobbling of the lower lip before the upper one reasserted control. Just as well. Britain would have struggled in the Second World War if everyone had gone around feeling sorry for themselves.

When Richard Hillary was badly burned after being shot down in his Spitfire in 1940, he ended up in what he euphemistically called 'The Beauty Shop' or, to give it its prosaic title, the Queen Victoria Hospital, East Grinstead, in the care of the pioneering plastic surgeon Archibald McIndoe. Another member of McIndoe's 'Guinea Pig Club' was a bomber pilot called Tony Tollemache who, like Hillary, had suffered severe burns to his hands and face in a crash.

When the pair were allowed out of hospital for the first time, they headed to a fashionable restaurant in London and 'surveyed the youth and beauty around us'. For a moment, Richard was melancholic; what young woman would ever find his melted face attractive? 'Here we are enjoying all the pleasures of old men at sixty,' he remarked to his friend.

'Speak for yourself,' retorted Tony. 'I am nearly the man I was. For you, there is still a little time, not much, but a little. Let us then enjoy ourselves while yet we may. Waiter, more brandy!'

For prisoners of the Japanese, humour was a little flicker of humanity that could not be extinguished, no matter how ghastly their existence. Ronald Searle was imprisoned at Changi, and was put to work building the Death Railway, where more than 12,000 Australian, British, Dutch and American prisoners died, as well as nearly 90,000 Asian workers. One of Ronald's fellow POWs, Australian Russell Braddon, described his English friend as 'covered from head to foot in a foul, creeping skin disease . . . his innards were torn with dysentery and his left hand – his drawing hand – holed with ulcers'.

He fell into a coma and Braddon waited for Ronald to die. But he didn't. He woke and immediately started drawing. He sketched everything; his forte was cartoons, which Braddon said were a 'delight'. They made everyone laugh, including the guards, who, in return for eggs, asked Ronald to draw them dirty pictures.

Death was also routine at the Chungkai camp but, remembered Colonel Cary Owtram, the British camp commandant, 'The aptitude of British troops for finding humour in circumstances of adversity is one of their most priceless possessions and, on numerous occasions, it showed itself during our imprisonment at times when life was most uncomfortable.'

Owtram was a regular army officer from an upper-middle-class family and he admitted that some of the humour he considered 'rather crude'; but still it made him laugh, and shake his head at the incorrigibility of the men under his command. He gave one example, when the low-lying parts of their camp were flooded one afternoon during the rainy season. Though emaciated, the POWs worked furiously to relocate the 'essential services' of the latrine pit, cookhouse and urinal pit on the one and only patch of high ground. Once done, a sign was erected on the high ground, mimicking the ARP (Air-Raid Precaution) signage back in Blighty. It read: 'ARP centre – Arseholes, Rissoles and Pissoles'.

* * *

Though the humour wasn't to Owtram's taste, he still found it funny. Those were the days. In modern Britain, humour is a minefield and one wrong quip could see a career go up in smoke. No one is safe and every one seems to find something offensive. It's a twenty-first-century phenomenon, one accelerated but not initiated by social media. As far back as 2001, the broadcaster Anne Robinson was the subject of a police investigation for describing the Welsh as 'irritating' in a comedy programme. In 2018, the journalist Rod Liddle also incurred the wrath of the Welsh for making a joke, this time about their language. Describing herself as 'incensed', Liz Saville Roberts, a Plaid Cymru MP, said, 'Whether you describe this as racist or not, it is prejudice and is being used against us as Welsh people.'

Was it racist? Was it prejudice? Or was it just a joke that wasn't to everyone's taste? That's the thing about humour, it's like food, and we all have our likes and dislikes.

Liddle and Robinson did still work again, which wasn't the case for the eminent professor (and Nobel Prize Winner) Sir Tim Hunt, whose career was ruined in 2014 when he made a sexist joke in a lecture; it was a crass quip but Hunt meant no harm by it. But within forty-eight hours, he was a pariah and the sanctimonious Puritans set off in search of another scalp.

So bad had the situation become by 2018 that Shane Allen, the BBC's Controller of Comedy, warned that a 'Victorian moral code' threatened British comedy. 'We live in an age where social media can bring comic material to people out of context,' said Allen. 'This means a handful of comments or opinions can quickly be taken out of context, which is damaging for a genre which is there to test boundaries and challenge orthodoxies.'

Allen's comments were somewhat undermined by the fact that he also said on his watch that a comedy such as

Monty Python would not have been commissioned because it featured 'six Oxbridge white blokes'. Instead, he wanted comedy comprised of a 'diverse range of people who reflect the modern world'. One of the Pythons, John Cleese, riposted that Allen was guilty of 'social engineering'.

Social engineering is certainly the strategy of the self-righteous offence-takers who prowl social media; they want to de-platform or 'cancel' anyone whose humour is unacceptable to their narrow world view. It cuts across the political spectrum leaving a small strip of comedic no-man's land for those whose humour is observational. But even that is fraught with risk. In 2019, Olaf Falafel won the best gag award at the Edinburgh Fringe Festival for this: 'I keep randomly shouting out "Broccoli!" and "Cauliflower!" – I think I might have florets.'

Suzanne Dobson, the chief executive of Tourette's Action in the UK, was outraged. 'Humour is a great way of educating people – but not only is it not funny to poke fun at people with Tourette's, it's not even that funny a joke, is it?'

Is it humour's job to educate, or is it to help us navigate the pleasures, pitfalls and problems of life? Probably best to keep school for education, and fringe festivals for comedy.

During the war, the Greatest Generation laughed at life and the people in it, and from it emerged a new humour, anarchic and absurd, far more edgy than the generally bland humour of the 1930s. Spike Milligan, Harry Secombe, Peter Sellers and Michael Bentine, who starred in *The Goon Show*, had all served in the war, and the wild girls of St Trinian's were the fruit of Ronald Searle's imagination. 'They say that I was partly the father of black humour,' said Ronald when he appeared on *Desert Island Discs* in 2005. 'But if you have that experience [of being a POW], you have to have a public that can accept it, and the fact that this humour suddenly was accepted, in a big way, meant basically that the attitude towards humour had changed.'

Then came the 1960s and another change in British humour with the anti-Establishment satirists. Beyond the Fringe in 1960 were the pioneers of this new comedy that attacked not just the Establishment but British culture in general, including the stiff upper lip of the wartime generation.

In the same decade, the British character underwent a subtle transformation; selflessness was replaced by selfishness in some as the 'Me Generation' emerged. The self-centred are rarely self-deprecating. The Greatest Generation laughed at themselves; Baby-Boomers had a tendency to take themselves seriously. Furthermore, as life grew more comfortable for Britons in the 1980s, the adversity that had been the basis of so much stoic humour disappeared.

Then came the risk-averse society, reared in a culture of fear, and out of it, Millennials, whose first instinct when faced with adversity is not to quip but to quail.

Once, it was Middle England that was quick to take offence at edgy humour – 'Disgusted of Tunbridge Wells', as the stereotype went – but now it's just as likely to be 'Outraged of Islington' with the left just as touchy as the right.

The lockdown made something of a celebrity of twenty-seven-year-old Will Hislop for the simple fact that he was one of the very few comics to mock the many examples of extreme behaviour induced by the pandemic, notably the 'Clap for Carers' ritual that became almost North Korean in its conformity. Most of Hislop's peers toed the comedy establishment line, their humour as well as their hands doused in antiseptic.

But who can blame them when the Gag Gestapo are so diligent? They were busily patrolling social media even during the lockdown, with the *Daily Mirror* accusing the cabinet minister Anne-Marie Trevelyan of 'stoking racial tension' after she joked on one platform that she had just received her COVID-19 rapid test kit from China – it was a fortune cookie with the message: 'You not have COVID-19'.

'China has sent twenty-two million pieces of PPE and 1,000 ventilators to the NHS,' the *Mirror* reminded its readers, forgetting to add that China also sent Britain COVID-19.

When the first Gulf War began in 1991, the BBC swiftly axed the comedy film *Carry On Up the Khyber* from its schedule because it feared viewers would be offended by the sight of the 3rd Foot and Mouth Regiment lifting their kilts to Muslim warriors. More recently, the episode of *Fawlty Towers* in which hotel guests are enjoined not to 'mention the war' has been taken off our screens – and then quickly reinstated with a warning about 'offensive material' – from the BBC's UKTV streaming service because it was considered offensive to Germans.

The BBC decision to can *Carry On Up the Khyber* staggered the novelist George MacDonald Fraser, a teenage infantryman in the Second World War. 'One couldn't help recalling the delight with which wartime audiences hailed movies which. . . . made merry of the struggle against the Nazis,' he wrote in *Quartered Safe Out Here*. 'No one took the war less seriously because of such entertainments; they did not offend taste, and far from undermining morale, they strengthened it. Times, and perhaps the sense of humour, have changed.'

The ribald and irreverent sense of humour recalled by MacDonald still exists but it's now under constant attack in an age of tyrannical puritanism. These sanctimonious killjoys have been in Britain for centuries; indeed, Noel Coward fell foul of them in 1943 when his song, 'Don't Let's Be Beastly to the Germans', was banned from the airwaves. Coward had to explain that he wasn't a cheerleader for Hitler; on the contrary, he was mocking a small minority of Britons who really did believe the Führer was receiving an unfair press. 'It was a satire, and as vitriolic and bitter a satire as I could well make it,' said Coward in October 1943.

'It was a satire on a trend of thought that I felt was once more beginning to spread within the minds of our moralists and sentimentalists; a trend of thought infinitely dangerous to the future of our country.'

The difference now is that the Puritans are growing in number and influence, and their objective of eradicating all 'inappropriate' humour is in danger of being accomplished.

Even Prince Harry has been 'puritanised'; once known for his *joie de vivre*, he now spends an increasing amount of his time lecturing the British people from his Los Angeles mansion about their privilege and the ills of their country's past. Yet this is the same Harry who, in 2006, went to a party dressed in a Nazi uniform. The party was fancy dress, and the young prince was just letting his hair down – it's what twenty-year-olds once did in Britain. The moral outrage that greeted his choice of costume was pathetic, with no one more pompous than the then leader of the Conservative Party, Michael Howard. 'It will cause a lot of offence,' he remarked. 'I think it might be appropriate for him to tell us himself just how contrite he now is.'

I asked Bob Lowson what he thought of the furore. After all, as a former commando and SAS soldier, he had spent five years fighting the Nazis, and a bullet from one of their snipers in April 1945 had left him with a lifelong limp. Was he offended?

'He looked very smart!' replied Bob, with a laugh. 'Why don't they leave the kid alone? It was just a bit of fun.'

12

Forgiveness

John Fowler was a survivor of the Blitz. We met in the summer of 2004 at his home on the south coast and John, then 77, told me his story. Although a tale of tragic loss, he told it without rancour, relating the facts in an honest and thoughtful manner.

He began with his recollection of 10 May 1941, a night he remembered well because it was out of the ordinary. It was the air raid that marked the end of the Blitz, the end of nine months of bombing that had killed 20,000 Londoners and seriously wounded more than twice that number.

That wasn't the reason that night stuck in John's mind. He recalled the day because he was back in London; on the morning of 10 May, he arrived at Waterloo Station on a train from Haslemere in Surrey. His mum and dad were waiting for him at the barrier for a tearful reunion.

John, fourteen, and his little sister Joan had been evacuated from their home in East Surrey Grove, Peckham, on 2 September 1939. They should have both gone to Haslemere but an administrative bungle resulted in Joan being evacuated to Sturminster Newton in Dorset.

John loved his new life in the countryside. Working on a farm was 'freedom' and he returned to London only because his sister was about to celebrate her thirteenth birthday. The family planned to take the train to Dorset on Sunday.

The Luftwaffe derailed those plans. Waterloo Station was badly damaged on the night of 10 May, as was the house of John's cousin, Rose, who spent two days under what remained of her home before finally being freed from the rubble.

John, who had been to the cinema with Rose earlier that Saturday evening, couldn't get back to Haslemere quickly enough.

The following year, John's sister returned to live in Peckham. She had adapted less well to life in the country, but her brother remained on his farm, enjoying life more than ever, despite the fact that peace had returned to London. John did pay a brief call home on Saturday, 15 May 1943 to wish his sister a happy birthday. He was back in Haslemere on the Sunday.

That same evening, 617 Squadron attacked the Möhne, Eder and Sorpe dams, dropping the 'bouncing bombs' of

Barnes Wallis that caused considerable flooding in the Ruhr valley. An outraged Adolf Hitler demanded immediate retaliation for the 'Dambusters raid', and it was delivered on the night of 17–18 May when the Luftwaffe swooped on south London. One bomb landed on top of 111 East Surrey Grove . . . killing John's father, mother and sister, Joan.

The rage didn't leave John for a number of years. 'I would've killed any German I met,' he admitted. But as he grew into adulthood, John understood that to carry the anger through life would only allow it to fester. It could heal only through forgiveness. 'I don't bear any resentment now,' he said. 'It was just one of those things that happen in war.'

Gladys Shaw was also caught in the air raid of 10 May 1941 while working as a first-aider in Peckham. The next day, a Sunday, she held her regular Sunday School class in St Mary's Church. Her theme was 'Love Thy Enemy'. 'I tried to make the children know that it was war that was wrong and that the airmen who had done the bombing had mothers, too, just like they did,' she said. At the end of the Sunday School, Gladys led the children in a prayer for the Germans.

Bobbie Tanner, quoted often in this book, also bore the Germans no grudge, although her forgiveness wasn't of the religious kind but a facet of her generous nature. 'I had no animosity towards the Germans,' she reflected. 'The pilots were doing their job and ours were doing theirs.'

The Nazis who ran the concentration camps weren't doing their job of fighting a war; they were engaged in a genocide, murdering millions of Jewish men, women and children. How could one forgive the people responsible for the death of six million Jews?

Eva Mozes Kor and her ten-year-old twin, Miriam, arrived at Auschwitz from Romania in 1944 and were subjected to medical experimentation by Dr Josef Mengele. Despite all their inhuman treatment, they were one of the very few sets of twins to survive 'The Angel of Death's' experiments.

In 1995, to mark the fiftieth anniversary of Auschwitz's liberation, Eva exchanged testaments with Dr Hans Munch, one of Mengele's medical assistants during the war. He signed a statement verifying the existence of the gas chambers, something Eva would be able to show any future Holocaust denier. In return, she gave Munch a 'Letter of Amnesty' in which she forgave him his crimes. On signing the letter, Eva 'immediately felt that all the pain I carried around for fifty years was lifted from my shoulders. The souls of millions of people [murdered there] were my witnesses. I immediately felt very free, emotionally liberated.'

The same cathartic release was experienced by Bill Moylon when he forgave the Japanese for the cruelty they had inflicted on him and his fellow POWs as they built the Burma Railway. 'When I got back from the war, there was so much anger,' he explained. 'But I couldn't hold on to my anger, I had to let it go. You can't visit the sins of the fathers on to the children . . . I have no ill-feeling against the Japanese at all.'

Bill visited Japan as part of the International Friendship and Reconciliation Trust and, in 2012, was present when the Japanese ambassador to the United Kingdom, Keiichi Hayashi, unveiled the Hiroshima Memorial Stone at the National Memorial Arboretum in Staffordshire. The driving force behind the memorial stone was Major Philip Malins, himself a prisoner of the Japanese and also a former chairman of the International Friendship and Reconciliation Trust. He died before the stone was unveiled but, on its inauguration, Mr Hayashi honoured the major's spirit of forgiveness and said, 'As I witness the monument, I feel even more compelled to pass his torch, his message of reconciliation and peace on to the younger generation.'

* * *

The noble message of Major Malins and the ambassador has been passed to the younger generation, but many don't wish to listen. Britain – and the West in general – is experiencing an age of unforgiveness and anger. 'A CULTURE OF CONDEMNATION HAS REPLACED CHRISTIAN FORGIVENESS,' ran the headline in the *Catholic Herald* in February 2019, regretting what the paper called the 'passion for vengeance' that now pervades Western society. The paper chronicled the witch hunts against several high-profile personalities (many of whom had committed no actual crime) and contrasted them with the Dutch woman Corrie ten Boom who, in 1947, shook hands with the guard who had tortured her in Ravensbrück concentration camp.

The conservative thinker Douglas Murray echoed the *Herald*'s sentiment in an article for the *Spectator* in June 2020. Lamenting the defeat of liberalism by 'woke' illiberalism in Great Britain, Murray wrote: 'Where the liberal mind is capable of humility, the woke mind is capable of none. Where the liberal mind is able to forgive, the woke mind believes that to have erred just once is cause enough to be "cancelled". And while the liberal mind inherited the idea of loving your neighbour, the woke mind positively itches to cast the first stone.'

Who or what is responsible for fostering an epoch of unforgiveness? The usual suspect – the Internet. Social media was meant to bring us together, but it has driven us apart.

In 2014 the Anglican priest and BBC broadcaster Giles Fraser predicted in the *Guardian* that 'the internet generation will be a lot better at forgiveness than older people'. This, posited Fraser, was because the Internet left a trial of past indiscretions so that, in future, it will not be possible to forget. 'Forgetfulness was always forgiveness for cowards,' he wrote. 'And I say "was" because, with the Internet, the age of forgetfulness is over . . . which means that we are going to have to learn to deal with our public figures as being more than bland, two-dimensional cut-outs'. He envisaged the dawn of a new era, one of honesty, acceptance and understanding. But, instead of Christian love, we've had bitter vengeance.

Indeed, a new phrase has entered the English language: 'offence archaeology', reputedly coined by an American writer, Freddie deBoer, in a 2017 essay entitled 'Planet of Cops'. The archaeologists dig deep into someone's past, determined to unearth an offensive remark so that they can be 'cancelled'.

This 'Cancel Culture', or the 'regime of censorship', as the British philosopher John Gray described it more pungently in a 2018 essay for the *Times Literary Supplement*, emerged from what he called a 'hyper-liberal ideology . . . that aims to purge society of any trace of other views of the world'.

Cancel Culture began in American and British universities but has spread now into wider society; it is built on intolerance, intimidation, malice and vengeance; on online petitions demanding X, Y or Z be sacked; on civil servants under siege in their own house by an angry mob; on journalists assaulted for their views and broadcasters sacked; on politicians heckled as 'Nazis' outside Parliament;

on actresses wishing the Prime Minister dead; on statues being demolished and war memorials vandalised, including that of Churchill, the man who inspired the free world's fight against fascism three-quarters of a century ago. There's no nuance in the narrow minds of these people; in this, they reflect the restrictive nature of Twitter. It's not a place for reasoned or in-depth debate. Space is limited so, to get noticed, to build up a following, you have to go to the extremes. Once there, it's hard to come back. You just move more to the left or the right.

In a 1937 essay, 'The Creeds of the Devil', Churchill warned against extremism, be it from the left or the right, saying: 'Let us not wander away from the broad, fertile fields of freedom into these gaunt, grim, dim, gloomy abstractions of morbid and sterile thought.'

But Britain has wandered away from these fields of freedom into a Cancel Culture that is a quasi-religion of fanaticism and unforgiveness. 'In institutions that proclaim their commitment to critical inquiry, censorship is most effective when it is self-imposed,' wrote John Gray. 'A defining feature of tyranny, the policing of opinion is now established practice in societies that believe themselves to be freer than they have ever been.'

Britain needs guidance from the Greatest Generation in order to navigate us through this turbulent period. The country is angrier and more divided than at any time in its recent history, a people riven by deep ideological differences. What's so disturbing is the refusal to compromise, to talk across the divides. Instead, we stand facing each other, trading stares and insults. This doesn't bode well for the future.

The Greatest Generation was confronted by an implacable enemy in 1939 and they triumphed after a long and exhausting struggle. At times, they needed guidance from a generation with more experience, a generation to whom, despite their differences, they listened and from whom they learned.

During the Blitz of 1940, a young lad in the Essex Home Guard saw the crew of a German bomber bale out of their aircraft. 'I've a good mind to get my rifle and shoot the bastards as they come down,' he said to his dad, a veteran of the Great War.

The man turned to his son, and told him, 'Never lose your humanity . . . or else you have nothing left.'